A Good Start

147 Warmup Activities
for Spanish Class

Rebekah Stathakis

First published 2011 by Eye On Education

Published 2013 by Routledge
711 Third Avenue, New York, NY 10017, USA
2 Park Square, Milton Park, Abingdon, Oxon OX14 4RN

Routledge is an imprint of the Taylor & Francis Group, an informa business

Library of Congress Cataloging-in-Publication Data

Stathakis, Rebekah.
  A good start : 147 warmup activities for Spanish class / Rebekah Stathakis.
    p. cm.
  ISBN 978-1-59667-165-2
  1. Spanish language—Study and teaching. 2. Spanish language—Spoken Spanish. I. Title.
  PC4065.S73 2010
  468.0071—dc22

                                                            2010035864

ISBN: 978-1-596-67165-2 (pbk)

Also Available from EYE ON EDUCATION

**Activities, Games, and Assessment Strategies
for the Foreign Language Classroom**
Amy Buttner

100 Games and Activities for the Introductory Foreign Language Classroom
Thierry Boucquey, et. al.

**CALLing All Foreign Language Teachers: Computer-
Assisted Language Learning in the Classroom**
Tony Erben and Iona Sarieva

**Differentiated Instruction:
A Guide for Foreign Language Teachers**
Deborah Blaz

Bringing the Standards for Foreign Language Learning to Life
Deborah Blaz

**A Collection of Performance Tasks and Rubrics:
Foreign Languages**
Deborah Blaz

Foreign Language Teacher's Guide to Active Learning
Deborah Blaz

Teaching Foreign Languages in the Block
Deborah Blaz

Classroom Motivation from A to Z
Barbara R. Blackburn

Rigor is NOT a Four-Letter Word
Barbara R. Blackburn

**What Do You Say When…? Best Practice Language
for Improving Student Behavior**
Hal Holloman and Peggy H. Yates

**What Great Teachers Do *Differently*:
14 Things That Matter Most**
Todd Whitaker

Acknowledgements

I would like to express my sincerest appreciation to all of the people who have helped make this book possible. I am so thankful for all the support from friends, family members, and colleagues. Specifically, I want to thank the following people:

My husband, Alex, for all the time he has spent helping me refine my ideas. He is a constant source of encouragement and support.

My parents, Paul and Karen Wrobbel, for providing feedback on my manuscript, teaching me the power of education, and always believing in me.

Donna Hattendorf and Lily Barcelona for being excellent teaching partners and colleagues. Their feedback and ideas helped me greatly improve this text.

Mr. Bob Sickles from Eye On Education for all his help transforming my ideas into this book.

Meet the Author

From an early age, **Rebekah Stathakis** appreciated the tremendous benefit of speaking another language. She spent the first 18 years of her life living in Costa Rica, Spain, and Venezuela. She has also traveled extensively in Europe and South America. As a young child, Mrs. Stathakis was a true bilingual as she learned to speak Spanish and English simultaneously and grew up in a multilingual environment.

Mrs. Stathakis attended Northwestern University in Evanston, IL, where she graduated cum laude with a degree in Secondary Education. As part of her honor's thesis, she studied teacher identity. Mrs. Stathakis went on to earn a master's degree in Educational Leadership from DePaul University. In 2007, Mrs. Stathakis was the first teacher in her school district to earn National Board certification.

Mrs. Stathakis is passionate about foreign language education and helping all students become multilingual. She has taught a variety of ages, from toddlers to college students, but especially enjoys working with middle school students. In addition to teaching, Mrs. Stathakis works with students in extracurricular activities; she piloted an International Club at her school, and *The Viking Voyager* yearbook she advised earned multiple national awards.

In 2006, Mrs. Stathakis earned national recognition as a Disney Teacher Honoree. She has also earned multiple awards for her presentations at state and regional conferences. A few of the topics she has presented on include, "Making Grammar Instruction Come Alive," "Vocabulary Toolkit," and "Creativity in the Classroom."

Contents

Puzzles and activities that require students to think visually

Beginnings and Endings...183
Activities that teach students about prefixes and suffixes

Calendar Index

Some of the exercises in this book naturally fit with specific months or seasons. This index lists topics that may be most appropriate for specific time periods.

Vocabulary Index

Reviewing and reinforcing vocabulary is often one of the main objectives teachers plan for their warmup problems. Many of the exercises in this text can be modified to focus on the vocabulary you are currently teaching or want students to review. The text provides a variety of ideas of how you can modify the activity to meet your instructional goals with your curriculum. If you are looking for activities to target vocabulary here are some to try:

Free Downloads

Many of the tools discussed and displayed in this book are also available on the Routledge website as Adobe Acrobat files. Permission has been granted to purchasers of this book to download these tools and print them.

You can access these downloads by visiting www.routledge.com/9781596671652 and click on the Free Downloads tab.

Introduction

How Can These Exercises Help Me?

We all want to start class off well. However, with taking attendance, checking in student passes, answering questions, and other distractions, it can be difficult. Warmup problems are an ideal solution to this situation. Establish a daily routine where students know they are expected to come into class on time and immediately begin working on their warmup problem. Post the warmup problem in the same place so that students can quickly find it and get to work. While students are working, you can take care of all the details that fill the first few minutes of class.

Effective warmup problems have to be engaging. If not, students will be easily distracted and you will have to spend your time reminding students to get to work. This book is filled with engaging, innovative, and fun exercises that will help you start class smoothly and enjoyably. When students are engaged in learning that is a true *Good Start* to your class.

These exercises should take between three and five minutes; enough time to get students immersed in Spanish without taking instruction time away from your regular curriculum. Furthermore, these activities should all reinforce, enrich, and supplement your curriculum.

For Whom Is This Book Designed?

The activities in this book are designed for *all* Spanish students! There are a variety of ways to modify these activities to meet the needs of beginning students, advanced students, or heritage speakers. These activities can be used with a variety of ages from middle school to adult learners. As you read through the activities, select the activities that will be most interesting to your students. Suggestions are provided for modifications to the exercises to make them appropriate for a wide range of Spanish students.

If you work with advanced learners or heritage speakers, you may find some of the puzzles and word games particularly appropriate for your students. Your students may also enjoy the games that are included in this text. During the games, you can help students refine their use of language and can include a written component to help students work on their writing skills. Games, word puzzles and other creative activities can help your advanced or native students truly enjoy using Spanish and develop a love of languages.

How Should I Use This Book?

The exercises in this book are grouped by topic (such as word games, cultural activities, and grammar). You do *not* need to complete the activities in order. Instead, browse through them and find an activity that sounds appealing or fits well with what you are teaching. Including the variations, there are more than 200 activities in this text—more than enough for every day of the school year. At times, an exercise will fit logically with another. In these cases, the instructions let you know which exercises are linked together.

Most activities include short directions that can be easily copied onto a chalkboard. Activities with lengthier directions include student handouts for photocopying or displaying on an overhead projector.

On pages xii and xiii you will find an index that includes two sections. There is a *calendar index* that lists which activities fit well with particular months or dates. A second section lists activities that can be used to teach or review the *vocabulary* you are studying.

Will These Activities Help Me Meet National Standards and the Performance Guidelines?

All of these activities will help you meet the national standards for foreign language instruction. On the description page for each exercise, you will find a listing of what standards that exercise targets. Most exercises target the three communication standards by engaging students in meaningful conversations and activities that require them to use language in a variety of ways.

Completing all of the exercises in the book targets the five Cs of foreign language instruction (Communication, Cultures, Connections, Comparisons, and Communities). The ultimate goal is to encourage students to become life-long learners as they discover the joy of learning (which also targets Standard 5.2).

The variety of activities included in this text will encourage students to use all three modes of communication (interpersonal, interpretive, and presentational) in meaningful and enjoyable ways. Tailor the activities to best meet your students' needs so that these activities will help your students progress in their foreign language performance.

Can the Activities Be Modified?

Throughout the description pages you will find two versions of each exercise. The first version is primarily in Spanish and the second includes directions in English. The first version is also sometimes more challenging or lengthy. Strive to use as much Spanish as possible with your students (and expect them to answer the questions in Spanish, too!).

Although there are two versions listed, there are myriad ways that you can fine-tune the activities to fit your students, your classroom, and your instructional goals. These activities are designed to spark ideas and your own creativity. The exercises give you an idea of some of the types of activities that are effective with Spanish students; make the activities your own and fit them into your curriculum. You know your students and your curriculum best, use these activities as a guide but modify them to best meet your needs and the needs of your students.

Are There Any Games?

Many of these activities can be completed in a game format. Some students are naturally competitive and enjoy that format. The directions generally include information about how to present the activity in a variety of ways (such as a team game, individual exercise, or game for small groups). Games can sometimes encourage student engagement; however, all of the activities can be completed without prizes or an emphasis on winning or losing.

Will These Ideas Require a Lot of Planning Time?

 The vast majority of these activities are ready to be implemented immediately—no planning time required! All you need to do is post the directions in a central location. However, a small number of activities do require preparation before class starts and these activities are marked with a clock symbol (see left). If preparation is required, the directions clearly label exactly what is required (such as photocopies).

I Want to Encourage Critical Thinking—Will These Activities Do That?

These activities are designed to be challenging and to encourage students to think critically and creatively. Students need to use higher order thinking skills with these activities. Throughout the exercises, there are strategies that students can use as they learn to approach different types of problems. These strategies provide scaffolding that can help students develop their problem-solving skills. Modify the activities to ensure that they are appropriately challenging for your students.

Conociéndonos

Activities that help you and your students
get to know each other better as well as
activities that help to acquaint students
with their classroom environment

1. Mi nombre en español

Versión 1:	Versión 2:
¿Cuál es tu nombre en inglés?	What is your name in English? Do you have a Spanish name?
¿Tienes un nombre en español?	If not, choose a Spanish name. It may be the translation of your name or any name you choose.
Si no tienes un nombre en español, escoge uno. Puedes escoger cualquier nombre que quieras. ¿Por qué te gusta ese nombre?	Why do you like that name?

Presentation Suggestion:

Consider displaying a list of common Spanish names in your classroom.

Solution:

Students' answers will vary. Depending on students' Spanish levels, try to engage students in discussions, in Spanish, about what names they like and why. Encourage students to ask each other questions as well.

Standards Targeted: 1.1 and 1.2

2. Mi apodo

Versión 1:	Versión 2:
Un apodo es lo que llaman en inglés un "nickname." ¿Tienes un apodo? ¿Por qué tienes ese apodo? Si no tienes un apodo, inventa uno. ¿Por qué te gusta ese apodo?	"Un apodo" is a nickname. Do you have a nickname? Why do you have that nickname? If you do not have a nickname, choose one. Why do you like that nickname?

Presentation Suggestion:

Some students may wish to choose nicknames that are variations on their given names (e.g., Juanito for Juan). Others may choose nicknames such as "el sabio," or names with some personal meaning. Consider having students discuss their "apodos" in small groups first and then with the whole class.

Variations and Additional Activities:

Have students create an "apodo" for a partner, instead of for themselves. Then, have students explain why they selected that "apodo" for their partners. As always, ensure that students understand your expectations and only select nicknames that are appropriate for a cooperative learning environment.

Standards Targeted: 1.1, 1.2, and 1.3

3. ¿Me crees?

Versión 1:	Versión 2:
Escribe tres oraciones que te describen. Dos deben ser oraciones verdaderas. La otra oración debe ser falsa.	Write three sentences about yourself. Two of the sentences should be true. One should be false.
Ejemplo:	Ejemplo:
1. Originalmente, mi familia es de Alemania.	1. Originalmente, mi familia es de Alemania.
2. Toco la guitarra eléctrica.	2. Toco la guitarra eléctrica.
3. El verano pasado viajé a Disneyworld.	3. El verano pasado viajé a Disneyworld.

Presentation Suggestion:

You may want to model this activity for the class using three statements about yourself. Students are often interested in learning fun facts about their teachers. If you include facts about yourself as the example, it might help students to quickly engage in the activity and fully understand the activity.

Once students have completed their sentences, you can play a short game. Have a student read her sentences for the class. Then, each student must write down which number is the false statement. If the students guess correctly, they give themselves a point. Select a few students each day and play this game three or four days in a row in order to get to know your class better. Make sure students alternate where they put their false statement (they shouldn't all make #3 the false statement when they read them aloud!).

Variations and Additional Activities:

Collect all of the papers and keep them in handy location. Whenever you have a spare moment, read a student's paper and have the class guess which statement is false. You can also have students explain why they think it is false and debate with each other. This is a nice activity for the last minute of class, when students finish an activity quickly, or on days when you need to help students transition back to class (like after a fire drill).

Instead of playing as a class, have students read their sentences in small groups (three or four students). Again, students should guess which statement is false. This variation ensures that all students will have more opportunities to speak. It also might be less intimidating if students aren't yet ready to share in front of the whole class. However, it doesn't allow everyone to get to know each other.

Standards Targeted: 1.1, 1.2, and 1.3

4. Un objeto precioso

Versión 1:	Versión 2:
Todos tenemos cosas que nos gustan mucho. A veces estas cosas no cuestan mucho y no tienen mucho valor para otras personas pero sí para nosotros. Describe tu objeto más precioso. ¿Por qué es tan precioso para ti?	Everyone has things that they really like. At times, these things may not cost a lot or mean much to others, but they are very valuable to us. What is your most valuable object? Why is it so valuable to you? Try to write as much as possible *en español*.

Presentation Suggestion:

Students may feel uncomfortable sharing about something so personal. They may feel more comfortable if given the opportunity to share in small groups or with partners. In addition, students may feel more comfortable if you provide them with an example. Students often appreciate the opportunity to get to know something personal about their teachers. If time permits, ask them to bring in a photo of their special object and then describe it for the class.

Standards Targeted: 1.1, 1.2, and 1.3

5. Mis cosas favoritas

Versión 1:	Versión 2:
¿Cuál es tu película favorita? ¿Por qué? ¿Qué tipo de película es? ¿Cuál es tu libro favorito? ¿Por qué? ¿De qué trata ese libro? ¿Cuál es tu animal favorito? ¿Por qué? ¿Dónde vive ese animal?	¿Cuál es tu película favorita? ¿Por qué? ¿Cuál es tu libro favorito? ¿Por qué? ¿Cuál es tu animal favorito? ¿Por qué?

Presentation Suggestion:

You may want to ask different questions based on what vocabulary you want to review or reinforce. Consider using this type of exercise each chapter focusing on the chapter vocabulary. This type of problem can be a great assessment tool at the beginning of the school year; you can learn about your students and also assess how much Spanish they know in an informal setting.

Depending on students' knowledge and skills you may want to have them interview each other. Encourage students to ask each other questions and then describe how their tastes are similar or different.

Standards Targeted: 1.1, 1.2, and 1.3

6. Mi futuro

Versión 1:	Versión 2:
¿En el futuro, que serás? ¿Por qué? ¿Cómo te ayudará el español en ese trabajo?	¿Qué quieres ser en el futuro? ¿Por qué? ¿Cómo puede el español ayudarte en ese trabajo?

Presentation Suggestion:

There are a variety of ways to present this depending on what verb tenses your students know. You can use the present-tense (such as used above in Versión 2) by using verbs like "quieres," "piensas" or "vas." For students who are more advanced, you can use the future (as in Versión 1) or conditional (as in "gustaría").

After the problem, you may want to provide a sample answer so that students can see how to structure their response. This is especially useful for beginning students who may forget how to conjugate the verb in their response.

Solution:

Students' answers will vary. Encourage students to think about creative ways to use Spanish in their chosen careers. For example, they might be able to travel overseas to a Spanish-speaking country with their work. They might find a job where they would work in or with a Spanish-speaking community. They might work as translators in an interesting field (e.g., as the team translator for a baseball team). This can be a wonderful opportunity to sell students on some of the many benefits of mastering another language!

Variations and Additional Activities:

Collect the student responses. Read a response without divulging who wrote the answer. Then have students in your class vote on who they think wrote the answer. If you want to turn this activity into a game, award a point each time a student correctly guesses who wrote an answer. At the end, the student with the most points wins.

As a followup or alternate activity, ask students to each select a person from the class to be their partner. Then have the students write a paragraph describing what strengths they think their partners have and what occupations they would be well-suited for. Encourage the students to list multiple positive attributes for their partners and explain how those attributes would contribute to appropriate careers. Also, require the students to think about how their partners could use Spanish in these different careers.

Standards Targeted: 1.1, 1.2, 1.3, 3.2, 5.1, and 5.2

7. Descríbete

Versión 1:	Versión 2:
Escribe tu nombre en el lado izquierdo de tu hoja. Ahora, encuentra un adjetivo para cada letra de tu nombre. Usa adjetivos que te describen.	Write your name down the left side of your paper. Now, find an adjective (in Spanish) for each letter of your name. Use adjectives that you think describe you.

Ejemplo:

M – magnífica
A – amable
R – responsable
I – inteligente
A – alegre

Ejemplo:

M – magnífica
A – amable
R – responsable
I – inteligente
A – alegre

Presentation Suggestion:

Students may have difficulties finding adjectives for letters that are uncommon in Spanish (such as K, W, or X). If students use Spanish names, they will probably find this exercise much easier to complete. For advanced/native students, ask them to write a sentence explaining why they think each adjective is appropriate.

Variations and Additional Activities:

Ask students to complete an acrostic for a class partner, famous person, or relative. Encourage students to write sentences explaining why they feel the adjectives they chose are appropriate. Students can then share their acrostics with the people they describe.

Solution:

Students' answers will vary. Make sure that students change the gender of the adjectives, as appropriate.

Standards Targeted: 1.1, 1.2, and 1.3

8. ¡Yo también!

Escribe una lista de hechos sobre ti mismo. Quieres escribir cosas que probablemente tienes en común con otras personas en las clase. Cuando compartimos las listas, vas a recibir un punto por cada cosa que tienes en común con otra persona.

Ejemplo: Tengo una hermana.

Write a list of facts about yourself. You want to write things that you think you have in common with other people in the class. When we go over your list, you will earn a point for everything you have in common with someone else.

Ejemplo: Tengo una hermana.

Presentation Suggestion:

The directions for this warmup are a little long so you may want to go over them quickly with your students. After students have a few minutes to write their statements, go over them with the whole class. Depending on how much time you have, you might only pick three or four volunteers. As they read their statements aloud, have their classmates say "yo también" if the statement is true for them, too. If you want to turn this into a game, students earn one point for every classmate that agrees. At the end of a certain number of statements (three or four), the winner is the person with the most points.

This game can help students think about the different things they have in common. This can create more of a collaborative environment when students realize that they share a lot in common even with people they don't know well or don't particularly like.

Variations and Additional Activities:

Have students go over their statements in small groups. Again, you can award points based on number of matches. Then, there would be a winner in each group.

Add the rule "No statements about things we can see." This makes the activity a little more challenging and removes statements like "Tengo pelo." Sometimes, students will start listing all their physical attributes and never consider other topics.

To review the chapter vocabulary, require that students include one vocabulary word (in a meaningful way) in each of their sentences. You can use this simple game with each chapter; it is a fun way to use the vocabulary and get to know your students better.

Standards Targeted: 1.1, 1.2, and 1.3

9. Firmas

Preparation:

Make copies of the student worksheet.

Description:

This activity requires students to ask questions of their classmates in order to find target sentences.

♦ First, you will need to make enough photocopies of the "Firmas" handout for all of the students in your class.

♦ Students should begin by reading the directions and the statements.

♦ Then students should go up to classmates and ask them questions in Spanish. If a classmate truthfully answers with one of the statements, s/he should then sign the line next to the statement.

Example: The statement on the papers says, "Me gusta comer cereal para desayuno." Peter walks over to Omar and says, "¿Qué te gusta comer para desayuno?" Omar responds with the target sentence so Peter says, "Firma, por favor" and Omar signs next to the target sentence.

♦ Students can only have a classmate's signature once. Peter cannot continue talking to Omar and have Omar sign five of his statements. The goal is for students to have the opportunity to talk to many different students and not just their friends.

♦ The activity continues for a set amount of time (approximately five minutes).

♦ At the end of the time, students sit down. You can go through the statements and ask students who they had sign each statement. Then you can find out which student collected the greatest number of signatures.

Presentation Suggestion:

Depending on students' skills, you may want to review asking questions before beginning this activity. Encourage students to create questions in different ways:

♦ Use a question word such as qué, por qué, dónde or cómo.

♦ Make the statement and use inflection to convey that it is a question. In writing you would also include question marks at the beginning and end of the sentences.

♦ Put the subject of the sentence after the verb. For example,"¿Comiste tú la galleta?"

If this is the first time you have done an activity like this, you may need to model the activity before students begin.

Instead of using the twenty statements on the worksheet, you could personalize the statements with information about your students. Two days before this warmup, as homework, have students answer a number of questions about themselves. Then use their answers to create the list of statements. Create at least one statement for each student. You can tailor the questions to topics you are studying or things you want to review (e.g., you could ask questions about food preferences, life ambitions, or other topics).

Variations and Additional Activities:

By changing the statements, you can use this activity frequently to target a variety of grammar or vocabulary topics. This activity can also be a fun game you can include in your repertoire of classroom games. Compete to see who can be the first to collect all twenty signatures or give students a time limit. You can also give this activity as a homework assignment, although it is very difficult to ensure that students will speak in Spanish outside of the classroom.

Standards Targeted: 1.1, 1.2, 1.3, and 5.1

Nombre:_____ Fecha:_____

Firmas

Directions: Your task today is to collect as many signatures as possible. In order to get a signature, you must ask your classmates questions hoping they will answer with one of the following statements. If a classmate answers with one of the statements below, say "Firma, por favor" and they will sign the line next to the statement. Make sure that each person only signs your paper once. You want to try to get everyone to sign.

You will also answer questions (honestly!) for your classmates. If your answer matches one of the statements below, you will sign your classmate's paper.

_____ Mi cumpleaños es en septiembre.

_____ Mi clase favorita es la clase de matemáticas.

_____ Me gusta el invierno.

_____ Tengo 2 hermanos.

_____ Estoy cansado(a).

_____ Como el desayuno todos los días.

_____ Soy deportista.

_____ Sé tocar un instrumento musical.

_____ Me gusta bailar.

_____ Me gustan los refrescos.

_____ Veo la televisión mucho, por lo menos 30 minutos cada día.

_____ No me gusta la primavera.

_____ Mi deporte favorito es el fútbol.

_____ Tengo un perro o gato.

_____ No me gusta nada cantar.

_____ En mi armario tengo una calculadora.

_____ Estoy muy bien hoy.

_____ Mi cumpleaños es en mayo.

_____ Me gusta ir de pesca.

10. ¡Yo nunca!

Versión 1:	Versión 2:
Escribe dos oraciones empezando con "Yo nunca...." Piensa en cosas que probablemente no tienes en común con los demás en tu clase.	Write two sentences starting with the phrase "I never...." Try to think of things that are probably unique to you.
Ejemplo: Yo nunca como los plátanos porque no me gustan.	Ejemplo: Yo nunca como los plátanos porque no me gustan.

Presentation Suggestion:

Once students have written their sentences you can have them share with the class or in small groups. It can be enjoyable to see how unique each member of the class is. After each statement, you can have students respond saying "¡Yo tampoco!" Or, they can disagree and explain why (ejemplo: "¡Me encantan los plátanos! Los como casi todos los días."). This can be a fun time to teach them expressions such as "No puede ser" or "No me digas."

Variations and Additional Activities:

This activity can also be turned into a game. Students earn a point for their statement only if they are the only person who can truthfully give that statement. If there is a tie, students can write a third (or fourth) statement.

To review the chapter vocabulary, require that students include one vocabulary word (in a meaningful way) in each of their sentences. You can use this simple game with each chapter; it is a fun way to use the vocabulary and get to know your students better.

If your students have learned the present perfect tense, this is a perfect opportunity to review it! Change the warmup to say:

Escribe dos oraciones empezando con "Yo nunca he..." Piensa en cosas que probablemente no tienes en común con los demás en tu clase.

Ejemplo: Yo nunca he comido un plátano.

Para esta actividad necesitas usar el presente perfecto.

Standards Targeted: 1.1, 1.2, and 1.3

11. Todo lo necesario

Versión 1:	Versión 2:
En esta sala, puedes encontrar todo lo necesario para la clase de español. Fíjate en los detalles de esta sala y responde a las siguientes preguntas.	You should be able to find everything you need for class right in this room. Take a look around and answer the following questions. Try to answer using as much Spanish as possible.

Versión 1:

En esta sala, puedes encontrar todo lo necesario para la clase de español. Fíjate en los detalles de esta sala y responde a las siguientes preguntas.

1. Cuando entras en la clase, ¿qué debes hacer?

2. Si quieres usar el baño, ¿dónde están los pases?

3. Si no tienes un material importante (por ejemplo un lápiz o bolígrafo), ¿qué debes hacer?

4. ¿Dónde está la tarea?

5. ¿Dónde están los diccionarios?

Versión 2:

You should be able to find everything you need for class right in this room. Take a look around and answer the following questions. Try to answer using as much Spanish as possible.

1. When you walk into class, what should you do?

2. If you need to use the washroom, where are the passes?

3. If you are missing an important supply (pen, pencil, etc.), what should you do?

4. Where is the homework listed?

5. Where are the dictionaries?

Presentation Suggestion:

This exercise is ideal for the beginning of a new school year or term when you want to review some of your policies and procedures. This activity will help students quickly review how to best use their classroom environment. Select the questions that are relevant and modify or delete those that do not fit with your classroom.

Variations and Additional Activities:

Consider using this type of activity if you have a new student starting in your class. The students in your class can respond to these (or similar questions) and help educate the new student about your classroom rules and procedures. Furthermore, this will help your students review what they should be doing regularly and what materials are available in your classroom.

Standards Targeted: 1.1, 1.2, and 1.3

12. Verdadero o falso

Preparation:

Before class begins, write down five true/false statements about your classroom. Create a few sentences that will help your students use your classroom space effectively (e.g., include a sentence about where dictionaries are located or where you file class handouts). Also, if you do a little research, you may be able to find some very interesting trivia about your school or classroom. And, with a little creativity, you can make up some fun false statements! Sample statements include:

- ♦ En esta sala, hay 132 libros en el estante.
- ♦ En un día normal, 112 estudiantes usan esta sala.
- ♦ Hay una réplica de una pintura de Goya en la pared.
- ♦ Esta sala fue construida en 1979.
- ♦ Hace 20 años, Hilary Clinton estudió en esta sala.

You can include some statements that the students can actually verify by looking around and other statements that will force students to use their estimation skills.

Presentation Suggestion:

You can allow students to walk around the classroom as they verify statements or you can ask them to stay at their desks. Choose whatever will work best for your students and their needs.

Consider using this type of activity at the beginning of the year as a fun way to reinforce important information about your classroom and your class expectations. Use interesting false statements or engaging trivia to help pique students' interest.

Variations and Additional Activities:

Instead of true/false statements you could use a variety of different question types. Depending on your students' level, consider using short-answer questions or having students respond to the statements explaining why they believe they are true or false.

Standards Targeted: 1.1, 1.2, and 1.3

13. Algo nuevo

Preparation:

Before class begins, change something in the classroom; for example, display a new poster, change a bulletin board, or move a piece of furniture.

Versión 1:	Versión 2:
Atentamente mira alrededor de esta sala. Hoy, algo es diferente. Describe lo que es diferente.	Carefully look around the classroom. Something is different today. Describe what is different using as much Spanish as possible.

Presentation Suggestion:

Teachers dedicate a lot of time to preparing their classrooms. This exercise will help students learn to focus on their environment and (hopefully) learn from the instructional materials teachers post. You can use this exercise whenever you make changes to the classroom, such as a new bulletin board or different posters on the wall. This activity can also be a fun little game especially if you change something small!

Variations and Additional Activities:

An activity like this one can also be useful when you create a new bulletin board or display student work in your classroom. You can modify the activity in many ways. For example, consider creating a short list of questions that students need to answer using the materials you recently posted. You could ask questions about specific student work samples, posters, or information on bulletin boards.

Hidden Sombrero:

Hide a small "sombrero" (or any other object) on a poster, wall, bulletin board, or other place in your classroom. You can purchase sombrero stickers from a number of teacher supply companies or can select another item that you can easily find stickers of. If you prefer to not use stickers, you could draw a small object or use clipart.

Ask students to locate the sombrero and then describe where it is hiding. You could hide a small sombrero on displays or bulletin boards to help draw students' attention to the display. Establish a class tradition of finding hidden sombreros around the room. Consider providing a small reward to the first student to find a new hidden sombrero in the classroom.

Standards Targeted: 1.1, 1.2, and 1.3

Juegos con palabras

Word games that encourage creative thinking

14. ¡Buenos días!

Versión 1:	Versión 2:
¿Cuántas palabras puedes hacer usando sólo las letras en "Buenos días?"	How many words can you make using only the letters in "Buenos días?"

Presentation Suggestion:

Students may want to add or remove accents. For example, students may want to include "si" and "sí" because there is a difference with or without the accent. Decide what "class rules" you want for this activity.

Turn this into a game by competing to see who can come up with the most words. Also, you can have students work individually, with a partner, or in small groups.

Variations and Additional Activities:

You can change the phrase "Buenos días" and use any other word or sentence. It can be fun to use this warmup problem before a holiday or other special event and use a phrase related to that event. You can also do this problem having students use the letters in their full names.

As another game variation, have the first student who arrives in class pick 10 letters. You can pick the letters from Scrabble tiles, 3×5 cards with letters, or any other letterset you have available. The students have to create as many words as possible using those ten letters. Vary the number of letters used as appropriate for your students and their Spanish skills.

Solution:

There are many words that students can create including:

beso – kiss	nido – nest
boda – wedding	no – no
bueno – good	nos – reflexive pronoun for us
buen – good	nudo – knot
de – from	sano – healthy
día – day	sé – I know
nadie – no one	si – if
nado – I swim	sí – yes

Standards Targeted: 1.1, and 1.3

15. La cadena de palabras

Versión 1:

Hoy vas a hacer una cadena de palabras. La última letra de una palabra tiene que ser la primera letra de la próxima palabra. No se permite repetir palabras. ¡Sólo tienes un poco de tiempo y necesitas crear una cadena muy larga!

Ejemplo:

pensa**r** – relo**j** – jamón...

La primera palabra es:

Hol**a**

Versión 2:

Today, you are going to make a word chain. The last letter of one word must be the first letter of the next word. You cannot repeat any words. You only have a little bit of time to make the longest chain possible.

Ejemplo:

pensa**r** – relo**j** – jamón...

La primera palabra es:

Hol**a**

Presentation Suggestion:

You can change the first word to match a special occasion or topic you are studying. If students are struggling because they keep getting stuck on the same letter, remind them that they can make words singular or plural, feminine or masculine, and they can conjugate their verbs.

Variations and Additional Activities:

There are many variations to this simple game. You can have students compete individually to see who can have the longest chain. Length can be measured by number of words or total number of letters.

Alternately, students can play with partners or in small groups. The first student adds a new word and then passes the chain on to the next student. The student must add another word and pass the chain on. If a student cannot add a word (within a reasonable time frame) that student is eliminated. The goal is to be the last student remaining. This game can also be played as a whole class with a few teams. The teams take turns adding words. To make it more difficult on other teams, students should think of words that end in a difficult letter!

To make the game more challenging, add the rule that all words must fit within a given category. For example, all the words must be things that you could eat or all the words must be things that would fit in a locker. By adding this rule, you can focus on thematic vocabulary that you are studying or reviewing.

Standards Targeted: 1.1, 1.2, and 1.3

16. Palabras escondidas

Versión 1:	Versión 2:
En las siguientes palabras, otras palabras están escondidas. Encuentra las palabras escondidas, sin cambiar el orden de las letras.	In the following words there are other words hidden. Find the hidden words without changing the order of the letters.

Versión 1:

1. alrededor
2. canoso
3. bella
4. disfrutar
5. efectos
6. enamorado
7. globo
8. plata
9. restaurantes
10. servir

Versión 2:

1. alrededor
2. canoso
3. bella
4. disfrutar
5. efectos
6. enamorado
7. globo
8. plata
9. restaurantes
10. servir

Presentation Suggestion:

Instead of the ten words above, substitute words that you are currently studying or that you would like to review with students.

Solution:

1. alrededor = al, red, dedo, o
2. canoso = oso, os, o
3. bella = ella, a, la
4. disfrutar = fruta, a
5. efectos = tos
6. enamorado = morado, a, o, mora, amo
7. globo = lobo, o
8. plata = lata, la, a
9. restaurants = antes, a
10. servir = ser

Variations and Additional Activities:

As a followup activity, ask students to think of words that have hidden words inside of them. Encourage students to use the current vocabulary. Give students two or three minutes to think of their lists. Then, have them exchange their lists with a partner. Ask the partners to find the hidden words. Consider creating a huge class list of words containing hidden words. Students would write their words on a large poster-board and write the hidden words in a different color to visualize them easily. Alternately, consider giving students 3×5 cards to write their words on and then make a bulletin board with all of the words.

Hidden Word Clue Activity:

Create clues for a word with hidden word(s). You can use the examples below or create clues with your chapter vocabulary.

Examples:
1. lo que pones en tus pies
    un animal con pico
    Answer: za**pato**

2. idioma que aprendes
    365 días
    Answer: esp**añol**

3. no alto
    condimento popular en comida italiana
    Answer: b**ajo**

4. limpiar/organizar
    rectángulo de madera   que usas para medir cosas
    Answer: ar**regla**r

5. persona en un restaurante que trae tu comida
    donde duermes
    Answer: **cama**rero

After reading the clues, students need to think of the one word that answers both clues (as one of the answers is hidden inside of the other word).

As another activity, ask students to think of hidden words and write their own clues. After students write clues for three to five words, they should exchange their clues with a partner. Students must solve their partners' clues. Encourage students to discuss their answers in Spanish with their partners.

Standards Targeted: 1.1, and 1.3

17. Palabras mezcladas

Versión 1:	Versión 2:
Las letras en las siguientes palabras están mezcladas. ¿Puedes adivinar qué palabras deben ser?	The letters in the following words have been mixed up. See if you can unmix the following words.
Ejemplo:	Ejemplo:
zacaeb = cabeza	zacaeb = cabeza
Pista: todas las palabras tienen que ver con la escuela.	Hint: All of the words have to do with school.
1. cimaloh	1. cimaloh
2. atera	2. atera
3. marrioa	3. marrioa
4. silorb	4. silorb
5. acamutopodr	5. acamutopodr
6. forsepor(a)	6. forsepor(a)
7. tenastuides	7. tenastuides
8. zipál	8. zipál
9. caless	9. caless
10. taperca	10. taperca

Presentation Suggestion:

This problem can be a good way to review classroom words at the beginning of the school year. You can also use this exercise from time to time featuring the chapter vocabulary that you are studying. If students are struggling to unscramble a word, consider providing them with Spanish hints or clues.

Solution:

1. cimaloh = mochila
2. atera = tarea
3. marrioa = armario
4. silorb = libros
5. acamutopodr = computadora
6. forsepor(a) = profesor(a)
7. tenastuides = estudiantes
8. zipál = lápiz
9. caless = clases
10. taperca = carpeta

Standards Targeted: 1.1, 1.2, and 1.3

18. La telaraña

Versión 1:	Versión 2:
Vas a crear una telaraña de palabras. Vas a empezar con la palabra "empieza" en el centro. Puedes conectar palabras nuevas al principio o el fin de las palabras en la telaraña. Cuando conectas palabras tienen que tener una letra en común donde están conectadas. Por ejemplo, puedes conectar "agua" con el fin de "empieza" porque comparten la "a." Intenta crear una telaraña muy larga y ancha.	You are going to create a word spiderweb. You will start with the word "empieza" in the center. You can connect new words at the beginning or the end of a word. Wherever words connect they must have the same letter in common. For example, "agua" can connect to the end of "emp-ieza" because they would share the "a." Try to make your web as long and wide as possible.

ejemplo:

Presentation Suggestion:

The directions for this exercise are a little bit complicated so students may need to see the sample and go over the directions as a class. Students cannot repeat any words. If they get stuck on certain letters, remind them to use feminine or masculine, singular or plural, and to conjugate verbs.

Variations and Additional Activities:

Students can complete this exercise individually or with a small group. Students who are more competitive may want to see who can complete the largest web in a given amount of time. Other students may be happy to complete the exercise without any competitive element.

Challenge:

To make this exercise more challenging, students can only connect words if they can give a sentence (in Spanish, of course) explaining how the two words are connected. For example, students could connect "agua" with "animal" and say, "Un animal necesita agua para sobrevivir." This can be an opportunity to let students' creativity shine!

Standards Targeted: 1.1, 1.2, and 1.3

19. La escalera

Preparation:

(Optional) You may want to make copies of the sample "Escalera" and the student template (page 24).

Versión 1:	Versión 2:
En este juego, vas a cambiar, añadir o quitar una letra en una palabra. Cada vez que cambias una letra, la palabra debe ser una palabra nueva en español. Escribe una palabra en la cima de la escalera. Para bajar los escalones tienes que cambiar, añadir o quitar una letra, pero no te olvides de que la palabra nueva tiene que ser una palabra verdadera. Vas a tomar turnos bajando los escalones (cambiando una letra). Si un jugador no puede hacer una palabra nueva en español, está eliminado. La última persona que puede cambiar la palabra gana.	In this game, you are going to change, add, or subtract one letter of a Spanish word. Every time you change a letter, the word must be a new Spanish word. Start by writing a word at the top of the staircase. To go down a step, you need to change, add, or subtract one letter, but don't forget the word you make still has to be a real Spanish word. You will take turns going down the steps by changing the Spanish word. If someone cannot think of a new word (by changing one letter) he/she is eliminated. The last player left wins!
Si tienes tiempo, puedes jugar varias veces.	You might have time to play multiple rounds.

Presentation Suggestion:

Some students may plan to win by selecting a difficult first word (such as "zanahoria") thinking that no one will be able to change only one letter. However, by allowing students to add a letter the following student could pluralize the word ("zanahorias") and win. After a few rounds using this ineffective strategy students should realize it is best to use words that do have a variety of options for change.

Students can play in pairs or small groups. Alternately, the whole class could play by starting with the same first word and everyone competing individually to see who can complete the longest staircase.

Variations and Additional Activities:

Individual activity

Instead of having students do this activity as a group game, students can complete the activity as individuals. At the beginning of class, give each student a blank staircase. Select the first word for the whole class to use. Students should try to make their staircases as long as possible. At the end of three to five minutes, have students share their staircases and see what different words they used and what words they finished with. If you would like to add a competitive element, declare the student with the longest staircase the winner.

Missing Steps

In this followup activity, students need to identify which words could fit on an empty step on a staircase. To move down a step, you can only change one letter of a word. However, some of the words have been omitted. For example:

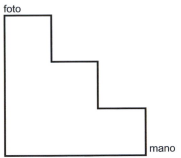

To solve this staircase, students could use "moto" and "mono" on the empty steps. Create a few staircases of varying lengths ahead of time, then omit a few words and ask students to fill in the empty steps.

Students can also create staircases with empty steps. Ask students to create a staircase with five to seven steps. Then, have students erase two or three words. Students should then exchange staircases with a partner and try to identify what words could fill in the empty spaces. Encourage students to use the vocabulary you are currently studying when completing their staircases.

Standards Targeted: 1.1, 1.2, and 1.3

Escaleras de palabras

Ejemplo:

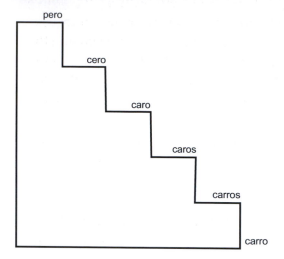

Escalera:

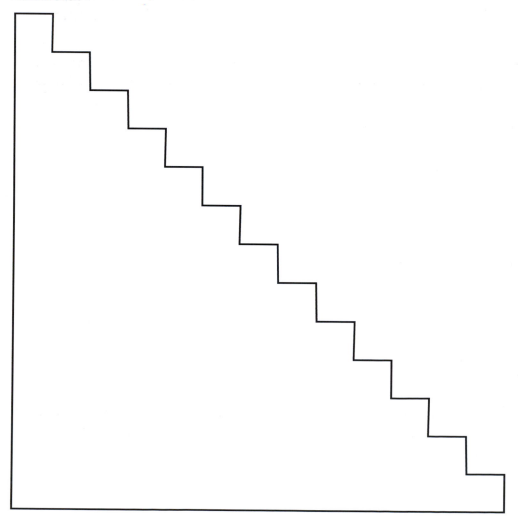

20. Palíndromos

<table>
<tr><td>

Un palíndromo es una palabra o frase que es igual del comienzo al fin o del fin al comienzo. Por ejemplo, puedes tomar la palabra "radar" y leerlo de la izquierda a la derecha o de la derecha a la izquierda y todavía dice "radar."

Las siguientes pistas describen palíndromos. Asegúrate de que todas tus respuestas sean idénticas de la izquierda a la derecha o la derecha a la izquierda.

1. Parte de tu cuerpo que usas para ver.

2. Ellos están en una piscina. ¿Qué hacen?

3. Una animal grande que vive en bosques. Duerme durante el invierno.

4. Un verbo: cuando ves a una persona y ya sabes algo sobre la persona.

5. Si tienes una lámpara y pones una bombilla de otro color tienes...

</td><td>

A palindrome is a word or phrase that is the same when read from the beginning to the end or the end to the beginning. For example, you can take the word "radar" and read it left to right or right to left and it still says "radar."

The following clues describe palindromes. Remember that each of your answers should be the same read from left to right or right to left.

1. Parte de tu cuerpo que usas para ver.

2. Ellos están en una piscina. ¿Qué hacen?

3. Una animal grande que vive en bosques. Duerme durante el invierno. Leones, tigres y...

4. Un verbo: cuando ves a una persona y ya sabes algo sobre la persona. En inglés es el verbo "to recognize."

5. Si tienes una lámpara y pones una bombilla (a bulb) de otro color tienes.

</td></tr>
</table>

Solution:

1. **ojo** Parte de tu cuerpo que usas para ver.

2. **nadan** Ellos están en una piscina. ¿Qué hacen?

3. **oso** Una animal grande que vive en bosques. Duerme durante el invierno.

4. **reconocer** Un verbo: cuando ves a una persona y ya sabes algo sobre la persona.

5. **luz azul** Si tienes una lámpara y pones una bombilla de otro color tienes...

Variations and Additional Activities:

As another activity, ask students to think of additional palindromes or try to write sentences that are palindromes. Some additional examples include: oro, somos, salas, la sal, and yo hago yoga hoy. Consider creating a bulletin board with palindromes. Students could also create clues for their palindromes and challenge partners or the class to identify a palindrome from a clue.

Standards Targeted: 1.1, 1.2, and 1.3

21. Rimas

Preparation:

Make copies of the student worksheet or use a projector to display the images.

Versión 1:	Versión 2:
Los siguientes dibujos son imágenes de rimas. Por ejemplo, este dibujo es de un tigre que está contento entonces es "el tigre alegre." Mira cada dibujo y escribe la rima.	The following pictures are drawings of rhymes. For example, the happy tiger would be "El tigre alegre." Look at each picture and try to figure out what the rhyme is.

Presentation Suggestion:

Instead of using the images provided, create rhymes that use the vocabulary you are currently studying or past vocabulary.

Variations and Additional Activities:

Have students create a picture rhyme for one (or more) of the chapter vocabulary words. They can use adjectives in the rhyme or create a rhyming sentence. Then, ask students to share their drawings and have the class identify the picture rhyme. Consider having students create their pictures on overhead sheets. Then, collect the sheets. Whenever you have a spare moment show one of the pictures to the class and see who can guess the rhyme. If overhead sheets are not practical, students can create the drawings on regular papers.

Game Variation:

Present the class with a picture rhyme. The first student or team who can guess the rhyme earns a point. At the end of the allotted time or a certain number of pictures, the team with the most points win. Alternately, present students with a set of vocabulary pictures and see who can guess the most rhymes given three minutes.

Matching Game:

In addition to creating the picture rhymes, consider requiring students to create questions or clues for their rhymes. For example, "¿Qué tienes cuando Winnie the Pooh come mucha miel?" Answer: "Un oso pegajoso." List the questions on the board and ask students to match the questions with the appropriate pictures. If time permits, have the students create their drawings (using vocabulary words) as the warm up exercise one day. Then, on the following day have them match the pictures with questions/clues.

Solution:

1. El conejo viejo
2. El oso pegajoso
3. La vaca flaca
4. Los peces franceses

Standards Targeted: 1.1, 1.2, and 1.3

Ejemplo: El tigre alegre (happy tiger)

1.

2.

3.

4.

22. Chiste: En la tienda

Lee el siguiente chiste. El remate (punch line) se trata de una frase en español que suena similar a una frase en inglés. Intenta ver si puedes identificar como se pueden confundir las palabras en español por inglés.

Un hombre español entra en una tienda de ropa americana. Él no habla inglés y el dependiente no habla español. El dependiente dice, "How can I help you?" El hombre responde, "Busco calcetines." Como no entiende, el dependiente le muestra diferentes artículos de ropa al hombre. "Do you want pants" dice, pero el hombre dice, "No, no quiero pantalones." El dependiente le muestra camisas, zapatos, corbatas y chaquetas pero siempre recibe la misma respuesta "no." Finalmente, le muestra calcetines y el hombre responde, "Eso sí que es." Exasperado el dependiente dice, "If you knew how to spell it, why didn't you tell me sooner!"

Read the following joke (chiste). The punch line is based on words in Spanish that sound like they might be English words. See if you can identify how the Spanish words might be confused for an English sentence.

A Spanish man walks into an American clothing store. He doesn't speak English and the clerk doesn't speak Spanish. The clerk says, "How can I help you?" The man answers, "Busco calcetines." Not understanding, the clerk starts showing him items. "Do you want pants" and the customer says "No, no quiero pantalones." The clerk shows him shirts, shoes, ties, and jackets always getting "no" as the response. Finally, he shows him a pair of socks and the customer replies "Eso sí que es." Exasperated the clerk says, "If you knew how to spell it, why didn't you tell me sooner!"

Presentation Suggestion:

To understand the joke, students may need to read it out loud to a partner. Then, they may be able to hear that to someone who doesn't speak Spanish "Eso" sounds like the letters "s" and "o," "sí" sounds like "c," "que" sounds like "k," and "es" sounds like "s."

Variations and Additional Activities:

If you have access to appropriate Spanish joke books, have groups of students read through the jokes together. Then, ask each group to select a joke they thought was particularly funny and share it with the whole class. If joke books are not available, there are numerous websites with Spanish jokes. However, you will need to ensure that students only access websites with clean, school-appropriate jokes.

Standards Targeted: 1.1, 1.2, and 1.3

23. Más chistes

Versión 1:	**Versión 2:**
Lee los siguientes chistes. Necesitas emparejar los chistes con los remates apropiados.	Read the following jokes and see if you can match the joke with the appropriate punch line.

Versión 1:

Lee los siguientes chistes. Necesitas emparejar los chistes con los remates apropiados.

1. En una carrera de peces, ¿quién llega último?

2. ¿Cómo sabes que la luna es mayor que el sol?

3. ¿Qué le dice el cero al ocho?

4. ¿Por qué llora el libro de matemáticas?

5. ¿Qué hace un pez cuando está aburrido?

A. Tiene muchos problemas.

B. El delfín

C. Porque la dejan salir de noche.

D. Nada.

E. Bonito cinturón.

Versión 2:

Read the following jokes and see if you can match the joke with the appropriate punch line.

1. En una carrera de peces, ¿quién llega último?

2. ¿Cómo sabes que la luna es mayor que el sol?

3. ¿Qué le dice el cero al ocho?

4. ¿Por qué llora el libro de matemáticas?

5. ¿Qué hace un pez cuando está aburrido?

A. Tiene muchos problemas.

B. El delfín

C. Porque la dejan salir de noche.

D. Nada.

E. Bonito cinturón.

Solution:

    1. B

    2. C

    3. E

    4. A

    5. D

Variations and Addition Activities:

Humor can be a great way to entice students to learn. These jokes (and the previous exercise) provide a very small sample of jokes you could use in your class. They use sheltered language that most students will be able to decipher. To maximize the value of this activity, consider finding jokes that use vocabulary you are studying or trying to review. There are a variety of resources you can use to find Spanish jokes, including joke books and websites. You may want to also establish a file of jokes that are related to the chapters and themes you teach (such as jokes about school, family, food). Then, you can easily use jokes that relate to what you are teaching and the vocabulary you are targeting.

Standards Targeted: 1.1, 1.2, and 1.3

24. La lengua de tecnología

Versión 1:	Versión 2:
Para escribir a máquina más rápidamente, usamos abreviaciones en nuestros correos o mensajes electrónicos. Por ejemplo, muchas personas saben que en inglés usamos "lol" para "laughing out loud" y "l8r" es para "later." Similarmente ahora hay un idioma de tecnología en español. Intenta escribir que significan las siguientes abreviaciones usadas en español:	In order to type quickly, we often abbreviate our language in e-mails and text messages. For example, most people know "lol" means "laughing out loud" and "l8r" is "later." Similarly, there is now a Spanish technology language. See if you can identify what the following abbreviations stand for:

Versión 1:		Versión 2:	
1. mdr	6. k	1. mdr	6. k
2. d+sia2	7. l100to	2. d+sia2	7. l100to
3. j+	8. na-	3. j+	8. na-
4. s	9. msj	4. s	9. msj
5. npn	10. kyat	5. npn	10. kyat

Presentation Suggestion:

Students may find it easier to identify the abbreviations if they try to say them out loud to a partner. For example, "l100to" makes more sense if you say it out loud with the number "cien" spoken. Encourage students to work with a partner while trying to sound out the words. Depending on students' levels, you may want to present these abbreviations in the context of a sample e-mail or message. Consider writing a simple message or set of messages for your students.

Solution:

1. mdr	muerto de risa (died laughing)	6. k	qué / que (what/that)
2. d+sia2	demasiados (too many)	7. l100to	lo siento (I'm sorry)
3. j+	jamás (never)	8. na-	nada menos (nothing less)
4. s	es (it/he/she is)	9. msj	mensaje (message)
5. npn	no pasa nada	10. kyat	callate (be quiet or shut up)

Standards Targeted: 1.1, 1.2, 1.3, 3.1, 4.1, 5.1, and 5.2

25. Tu lengua de tecnología

Cuando personas usan mensajeros electrónicos o correo electrónico, hacen nuevas palabras cortas para palabras o frases que usan a menudo. Por ejemplo, muchas personas usan "a2" para "adiós." Escribe algunas palabras que crearías para expresiones comunes en español.

Versión 2:

As people instant message and send e-mails, they create shortcuts for commonly used words or phrases. For example, people use "a2" for "adiós." What new words would you create for some common Spanish expressions?

Presentation Suggestion:

After students create their new abbreviations, have them write the words on the board and have classmates guess the meaning. You could also see how many students came up with the same words or phrase. Consider creating a bulletin board or poster featuring your new technology lingo.

Standards Targeted: 1.1, 1.2, 1.3, 4.1, 5.1, and 5.2

26. Un correo electrónico

Versión 1:

Ahora que sabes usar "la lengua de tecnología," escribe un correo electrónico a uno de tus amigos. Intenta usar las abreviaciones nuevas que aprendiste o inventa nuevas abreviaciones.

Versión 2:

Now that you have learned how to use "technology language," write an e-mail to one of your friends. Try to use the new abbreviations you learned or come up with some other ones.

Variations and Additional Activities:

After students write their e-mail messages, have them trade papers with a partner and respond. For a fast-paced activity, students can IM (instant message) each other and pass papers after one or two sentences. If you have white boards, students could write on them and pass them to their partners. Depending on your class environment, you may need to remind students that as a class activity, all their IMs or e-mails must be appropriate for school.

Standards Targeted: 1.1, 1.2, and 1.3

27. Sopa de palabras

Preparation:

Select chapter vocabulary words to include in the "sopa de palabras." Make sure you include subjects, verbs, objects, and other elements so students can create complete sentences.

Versión 1:	**Versión 2:**
Tienes que hacer oraciones completas usando las diferentes palabras de "la sopa de palabras." Asegúrate de que las palabras en tus oraciones estén en el orden correcto. Sopa:	Your goal today is to make as many sentences as possible using the different words located below in "la sopa de palabras." Make sure that you think carefully about correct Spanish word order. Sopa:

Presentation Suggestion:

It is up to you whether or not you want to allow students to change the conjugation of a verb or the ending of an adjective. Set your "class rules" and let students know your expectations.

Variation:

Have students compete to create the funniest, most interesting, or longest sentences.

Solution:

Answers will vary. You may want to have students check their sentences with a partner since there could be so many different right answers.

Standards Targeted: 1.1, 1.2, and 1.3

28. Los acentos importan I

Versión 1:	Versión 2:
Lee los siguientes grupos de palabras. ¿Qué significa cada palabra?	Read the following sets of words. What is the meaning of each word?
1. mas más	1. mas más
2. si sí	2. si sí
3. el él	3. el él
4. papa papá	4. papa papá
5. público publico publicó	5. público publico publicó
¡Los acentos son muy importantes!	Accents are very important!

Presentation Suggestion:

You may want to have students explain the meaning of the words in English or Spanish depending on their Spanish ability. You also could ask students to write sentences for the pairs that help demonstrate the difference between the words.

This is a good exercise to use if students tend to say things like, "Do accents really matter?" or "Isn't it close enough without the accent?" This activity helps students realize that they need to write carefully and pay attention to details (like accents).

Solution:

1. mas = but (conjunction)

   más = more

2. si = if

   sí = yes

3. el = the (masculine definite article)

   él = he

4. papa = potato

   papá = dad

5. público   = public

   publico = present-tense "yo" form of to publish

   publicó = past-tense "él/ella/usted" form of to publish

Standards Targeted: 1.1, 1.2, and 1.3

29. Los acentos importan II

Versión 1:	Versión 2:
Lee los siguientes grupos de palabras. ¿Qué significa cada palabra?	Read the following sets of words. What is the meaning of each word?
1. tu tú	1. tu tú
2. como cómo	2. como cómo
3. solo sólo	3. solo sólo
4. baile bailé	4. baile bailé
5. te té	5. te té
¡Los acentos son muy importantes!	Accents are very important!

Presentation Suggestion:

You may want to have students explain the meaning of the words in English or Spanish depending on their Spanish ability. You also could ask students to write sentences for the pairs that help demonstrate the difference between the words.

This is a good exercise to use if students tend to say things like, "Do accents really matter?" or "Isn't it close enough without the accent?" Hopefully, students will realize that they need to write carefully and pay attention to details (like accents).

Solution:

1. tu = your

   tú = you

2. como = as/ like or the present-tense "yo" form of to eat

   cómo = how

3. solo = alone (adjective)

   sólo = only (adverb)

4. baile = the dance

   bailé = past-tense "yo" form of the verb to dance

5. te = reflexive/ indirect object pronoun for you

   té = tea

Standards Targeted: 1.1, 1.2, and 1.3

El alfabeto

Games and activities that reinforce
the alphabet and specific sounds

30. Código

Versión 1:	**Versión 2:**
El siguiente mensaje está escrito en un código numérico (cada letra está representada por un número). Tienes que averiguar el código y traducir el mensaje. Después de traducir el mensaje tienes que escribir una respuesta. Escribe tu respuesta en español primero y después en código.	The following message is written in a numeric code (every letter is represented by a number). You need to crack the code and then translate the message. Once you have translated the message, you will need to respond. Write your response in Spanish first and then translate it into code.

Mensaje:

9–20–13–1. ¿3–20–15–1 8–24–23–1-24?

Código: Aquí está parte del código. Tienes que averiguar el patrón y resolver el código.

A = 1	CH = 6
B = 4	D = 5
C = 3	

Message:

9–20–13–1. ¿3–20–15–1 8–24–23–1-24?

Code: Here is the beginning of the code. See if you can figure out the pattern and crack the code.

A = 1	CH = 6
B = 4	D = 5
C = 3	

Presentation Suggestion:

If students experience difficulty solving the code, provide them with a few more letters from the code. If they are still struggling, encourage them to try to solve the code with a partner. Working through the puzzle orally may help them find the solution. Once students have solved the code, if they are struggling to decode the message, allow them to double-check their code with an answer key. That way, if they made a mathematical error, they can correct their code and finish the problem.

If some students finish very quickly, encourage them to write a message in code and pass it along to another student.

Additional Information:

The number of letters in the Spanish alphabet varies from country to country. In this exercise, the letters "ch," "ll," and "ñ" are included because La Real Academia Española considers them part of the Spanish alphabet. In 1994, the Real Academia did approve changing dictionaries and other documents to alphabetize "ch" and "ll" as entries under "c" and "l," respectively. However, La Real Academia still recognizes them as letters and they would be included in this type of code. Feel free to modify the code if you instruct students to use a different variation of the alphabet.

Variations and Additional Activities:

You can modify the code and use this activity multiple times. Students may also enjoy creating their own codes with partners and writing "secret" messages to each other. Keep the code relatively simple so students do not spend too long solving the pattern but instead can focus on creating a meaningful Spanish message.

As another variation, consider showing students Morse code. See if students can quietly tap a message to a partner using Morse code.

Solution:

Code:			Pattern
A	=	1	+3
B	=	4	−1
C	=	3	+3
CH	=	6	−1
D	=	5	+3
E	=	8	−1
F	=	7	+3
G	=	10	−1
H	=	9	+3
I	=	12	−1
J	=	11	+3
K	=	14	−1
L	=	13	+3
LL	=	16	−1
M	=	15	+3
N	=	18	−1
Ñ	=	17	+3
O	=	20	−1
P	=	19	+3
Q	=	22	−1
R	=	21	+3
S	=	24	−1
T	=	23	+3
U	=	26	−1
V	=	25	+3
W	=	28	−1
X	=	27	+3
Y	=	30	−1
Z	=	29	+3

Pattern:

For this code, students increase the number by three and then for the following letter decrease the number by one. They repeat this pattern for all the letters in the alphabet.

Translated sentence:

Hola.

9–20–13–1.

¿Cómo estás?

¿3–20–15–1 8–24–23–1-24?

Student Responses:

Student responses will vary but could include:

Estoy (muy) bien.

8–24–23–20–30 (15–26–30) 4–12–8–18.

Estoy mal.

8–24–23–20–30 15–1-13

Estoy así-así.

8–24–23–20–30 1–24–12—1–24–12.

Estoy cansado.

8–24–23–20–30 3–1-18–24–1-5–20.

Standards Targeted: 1.1, 1.2, 1.3, and 3.1

31. Viajando

Versión 1:	Versión 2:
ejemplo:	ejemplo:
Voy a **A**rgentina para comprar **á**rboles	Voy a **A**rgentina para comprar **á**rboles.
Voy a **B**arcelona para comprar **b**arcos	Voy a **B**arcelona para comprar **b**arcos.
¡Ahora es tu turno! Empezando con la A y llegando hasta la J, escribe una frase para cada letra. El lugar tiene que empezar con esa letra y lo que vas a comprar tiene que empezar con la misma letra.	Now it is your turn! Starting with the letter A and continuing through J, write a sentence for each letter. The place you travel to and the thing you buy both have to begin with the letter.

Presentation Suggestion:

Note: Completing the whole alphabet is time-consuming. Therefore, the alphabet is split so you do this activity two days in a row. If you would like to spend even less time on this activity, split the alphabet so that the activity takes three to five days.

Variations and Additional Activities:

There are many ways to do this activity. Feel free to modify the sentence depending on what you are studying. For example, use the past tense or change the subject for each sentence. In addition, instead of buying things in each place, substitute a verb such as "comer" or "ver." Also, instead of using actual place names, you could use places in a community such as "una escuela" for "e." This can be a great way to review different locations.

If time permits, begin at one side of the room and have the first student read his sentence for letter A. The second student would have to repeat the first sentence and add her sentence for B. Students continue and see how many letters they can get through as a class before forgetting the place/object. In addition, consider having students use the past tense to discuss other students' sentences. For example, the second student could say, "él viajó a Argentina para comprar árboles, yo voy a Barcelona para comprar barcos." This activity can be done with the whole class or in small groups.

Standards Targeted: 1.1, 1.2, and 1.3

32. Empieza con la letra...

Preparation:

Copy the activity cards or display on a projector. Included on page 40 are eight sample cards. Depending on how much time you want to spend, you can use one or more cards each day.

Versión 1:	Versión 2:
Lee las siguientes descripciones y escribe una(s) palabra(s) que encaja(n) con la descripción. Todas las respuestas para las descripciones en un grupo deben empezar con la misma letra. Algunas de las descripciones pueden tener muchas respuestas pero asegúrate de que todas las respuestas en un grupo tengan la misma primera letra.	Read the following descriptions and write a word that fits the description. For each of the five descriptions in a group, the words you identify should start with the same letter. Some of the descriptions may have more than one answer; you need to make sure that all of the answers in a group start with the same letter.

Ejemplo:

Versión 1:
- ♦ fruta verde o morada (**u**vas)
- ♦ opuesto de primero (**ú**ltimo)
- ♦ lugar para estudios avanzados (**univer**sidad)
- ♦ parte de tus manos (**u**nas)
- ♦ pronombre formal (**u**sted)

Versión 2:
- ♦ fruta verde o morada (**u**vas)
- ♦ opuesto de primero (**ú**ltimo)
- ♦ lugar para estudios avanzados (**univer**sidad)
- ♦ parte de tus manos (**u**nas)
- ♦ pronombre formal (**u**sted)

Presentation Suggestion:

Some students may quickly react by saying, "there are lots of words that fit!" Encourage them to list multiple words for each clue. Then they should look at their answers and find answers that have the same first letter. Students should also look at all the descriptions as some have only one or two possible answers. If they start with the more specific clues, they can identify a possible first letter.

Instead of using the cards included in this text, create your own cards that review and reinforce the vocabulary you are studying. Also, ask students to create cards to use for this activity. Students can create cards and then trade cards with other groups or students.

Variations and Additional Activities:

There are numerous ways to complete this activity. Students can work independently, with partners, or in small groups. You can go over the answers as a whole class or provide students with the answers so they can review their work with their partners or small groups.

The activity can also be completed as a game. Students form small groups. One student is the designated clue giver. The clue giver reads the first two clues. After the first two clues, if any of the players think they know the letter for the card, she can guess. However, if the player guesses incorrectly she is eliminated. If no one guesses correctly, the clue giver continues reading clues. After each clue, players can decide if they are ready to provide a letter guess; however, players are eliminated for incorrect guesses. The first player to correctly guess the letter wins.

Empieza con la letra…

Activity Cards

1.
- un símbolo redondo de amor y matrimonio
- ingrediente en una receta que añade mucho sabor; es común en comida española o italiana
- miembro de una familia
- cuando hace frío lo necesitas llevar
- bebida natural sin color

2.
- un postre popular en el verano
- una persona a quien puedes admirar
- un buen comienzo para una conversación
- una lista de cuando tienes que hacer diferentes cosas
- tienes esto antes de comer pero no después

3.
- vive en una biblioteca
- lo usas para abrir puertas
- reglas de un pais
- una fruta amarga
- los usas para ver cosas

4.
- tipo de jugo
- un ejercicio que haces en el agua
- tú, yo y ella (un pronombre)
- algunas personas se muerden
- las uñas cuando se sienten…
- cuándo sale la luna

5.
- como empezamos todos
- un color – no negro
- la casa de 32 cosas blancas
- deporte con 9 jugadores
- moverse al ritmo de música

6.
- mascota popular
- el fin de una carrera de estudios
- una palabra para describir a alguien que comparte a menudo
- nos hace reír
- una verdura verde

7.
- metal valioso
- animal o juguete
- un mes
- un lugar para trabajar
- qué haces con las orejas

8.
- animal o parte de una computadora
- color de pelo
- puedes comer aquí
- caja muy fría con comida
- un círculo con 12 números y dos manos

Solutions:

1. A
- anillo
- ajo
- abuelo
- abrigo
- agua

5. B
- bebé
- blanco
- boca
- béisbol
- bailar

2. H
- helado
- héroe
- hola
- horario
- hambre

6. G
- gato
- graduación
- generoso
- gracioso
- guisantes

3. L
- libro
- llave
- ley
- limón
- lámpara

7. O
- oro
- oso
- octubre
- oficina
- oír

4. N
- naranja
- nadar
- nosotros
- nerviosos
- noche

8. R
- ratón
- rubio
- restaurante
- refrigerador
- reloj

Standards Targeted: 1.1, 1.2, and 1.3

33. Usa cada letra

Las siguientes palabras no tienen todas sus letras. Necesitas completar las palabras usando cada letra del alfabeto solo una vez. Algunas letras del alfabeto no están incluidas en esta actividad.

A B C CH D E F G H I J ■ L LL M N Ñ
O P ■ R S T U V ■ X Y Z

ápi

In_lé_

_spa_ol

_arpeta _e argo_as

_ro_ecto

Mo_ _la

orari

Ti_er_s

P_o_esor

A_to_ús

Di_er_ido

E_a_e_

¿Sabes qué significa cada palabra? Si no lo sabes, usa tu libro o un diccionario para buscarlo.

Each of the following words is missing one or more letters. You need to complete the words by using each letter of the alphabet only once. A few letters of the alphabet are not included (they are blacked out).

A B C CH D E F G H I J ■ L LL M N Ñ
O P ■ R S T U V ■ X Y Z

ápi

In_lé_

_spa_ol

_arpeta _e argo_as

_ro_ecto

Mo_ _la

orari

Ti_er_s

P_o_esor

A_to_ús

Di_er_ido

E_a_e_

Do you know what each word means? If not, look it up!

Presentation Suggestion:

Some students may need additional guidance with this type of activity. Encourage students to begin with the easiest words. Then, for the words that they don't know, there will be fewer letters to choose from. Also, you can give your students the hint that all of the words relate to school. If the activity is still too challenging, consider providing clues for some of the words.

Solution:

Lápiz	Proyecto	Profesor
Inglés	Mochila	Autobús
Español	Horario	Divertido
Carpeta de argollas	Tijeras	Examen

Variations and Additional Activities:

This type of activity can be easily modified and used to target any vocabulary. Select a set of vocabulary words that you want to review with students. Then, try to omit each letter of the alphabet one time from the set. You may not be able to use every letter (for example, in this exercise the letters K, Q, and W are blacked out because they are not used in the words). For example, if you are studying food you could use:

A B C CH D E F G H I J ▉ L LL M N Ñ O P Q R S T U V ▉▉ Y Z

_ue_o	_is_e_
_u_v_s	Le_uga
J_días ve_ _es	A_o
Man_ana	P_ _a
A_cacho_as	_eló_
_o_o	P_ _o
_o_ur	

Answers:

Queso	Bistec
Huevos	Lechuga
Judías verdes	Ajo
Manzana	Piña
Alcachofa	Melón
Pollo	Pavo
Yogur	

As a followup activity you could also have students create this type of exercise. Then, they could exchange their lists with partners and try to complete the activity their partners created.

Game Variation:

Have students form small groups (three to five students). Give each group a Scrabble board game. If you do not have board games, you can write letters onto flashcards. Each set of letter flashcards should include multiple copies of vowels and common letters. One student should be the judge. The other students need to turn away while the judge sets up the game. The judge should create seven to ten words using the tiles/flashcards. Then, the judge will remove a few of the letter pieces and place them face-down in the middle of the table. The other players should then look at the words (with a few letters omitted). The first player turns over a tile/flashcard and must try to place it in one of the words. If the player is correct, s/he earns a point. If not, the tile/flashcard is passed on to the next player. Students take turns until all of the tiles/flashcards have been correctly placed in the words. If time permits, select a new judge and play again.

Standards Targeted: 1.1, 1.2, and 1.3

34. Todo el alfabeto

Versión 1:	Versión 2:
En el centro de tu papel, escribe el alfabeto empezando con la letra "A". Escribe solo una letra en cada línea. (Vas a llenar tu papel.) Ahora, tienes que pensar en una palabra para cada letra del alfabeto. Por ejemplo:	Write out all the letters of the alphabet going down the center of your paper. Every letter should have its own line. Then, think of a word that includes each letter of the alphabet and write it on that line. For example:
básquetbol bailar natación	básquetbol bailar natación
No puedes repetir palabras. La última regla es que todas las palabras tienen que tratar con el tema de **entretenimiento**. ¡Buena suerte!	You **cannot** repeat any words. Finally, all of the words must be related to the theme of **entertainment**. Good luck!

Presentation Suggestion:

You may want to provide students with an alphabet handout (see next page) so that they can start this activity more quickly. Modify the theme to fit with the vocabulary you are studying or wish to review.

After students finish, go over the words quickly as a class so that students can hear options for the letters that they couldn't fill. Also, you may want to say that the student who filled the most letters is the "winner."

Variations and Additional Activities:

This activity can also be completed as a game that students complete with partners or a small group. Each player takes a turn writing a word on the alphabet. Players can select any letter and do not need to complete the words in alphabetical order If a player cannot think of a word in a reasonable amount of time (twenty to thirty seconds), that player loses his/her turn. When time runs out, the player who wrote the most words wins.

Speed game variation:

Students play in small groups (three to four players). There is one alphabet handout and only one pen for the group. The first player writes a word on the alphabet and sets the pen down. The first player to grab the pen can add one word and then sets the pen down. Again, students race to grab the pen and add a word. At the end of the allotted time, the player who wrote the most words wins. Students can get very excited while playing this game; make sure that students understand your classroom expectations before beginning the game.

Standards Targeted: 1.1, 1.2, and 1.3

Todo el alfabeto

_____	a	_____
_____	b	_____
_____	c	_____
_____	ch	_____
_____	d	_____
_____	e	_____
_____	f	_____
_____	g	_____
_____	h	_____
_____	i	_____
_____	j	_____
_____	k	_____
_____	l	_____
_____	ll	_____
_____	m	_____
_____	n	_____
_____	ñ	_____
_____	o	_____
_____	p	_____
_____	q	_____
_____	r	_____
_____	s	_____
_____	t	_____
_____	u	_____
_____	v	_____
_____	w	_____
_____	x	_____
_____	y	_____
_____	z	_____

Rompecabezas

**Puzzles that will challenge your students
and force them to think critically**

35. Números y letras

Versión 1:	Versión 2:
En las siguientes oraciones, sólo está la primera letra de algunas palabras. Tú tienes que averiguar qué palabra debe estar en la oración.	In the following sentences, some words have been omitted, and only the first letter of the word remains. Try to find out what the correct words could be.
Ejemplo:	Ejemplo:
50 **e** en los **E.U.**	50 **e** en los **E.U.**
(50 **estados** en los **Estados Unidos**)	(50 **estados** en los **Estados Unidos**)
◆ **C** llegó a las **A** en 1492	◆ **C** llegó a las **A** en 1492
◆ 88 **t** en un **p**	◆ 88 **t** en un **p**
◆ 13 **r** en la **b** americana	◆ 13 **r** en la **b** americana
◆ 7 **c** en un **a i**	◆ 7 **c** en un **a i**
◆ 101 **d** en el cuento famoso	◆ 101 **d** en el cuento famoso

Presentation Suggestion:

Although some students may enjoy the challenge of this type of brain teaser, others may become quickly frustrated. Consider providing hints for questions that students are struggling with. For example you could tell students that "88 **t** en un **p**" has to do with a musical instrument. You might also want to encourage students to work with partners to brainstorm different ideas.

Solution:

◆ **Colón** llegó a las **Américas** en 1492

◆ 88 **teclas** en un **piano**

◆ 13 **rayas** en la **bandera** americana

◆ 7 **colores** en un **arco iris**

◆ 101 **dálmatas** en el cuento famoso

Variations and Additional Activities:

After students finish (or as a future activity) they could create their own sentences and challenge their classmates. At the end of each chapter or unit, you could encourage students to come up with a few of these problems utilizing the chapter vocabulary. Then, use the students' work as fun, challenging exercises if you have an extra moment, as an enrichment activity after a test, or as the next warm up.

This activity can easily be modified to fit with the chapter vocabulary or other content you wish to review or reinforce with students. Create your own sentences to fit with your curriculum and instructional goals. Some other samples include:

El Cuerpo:

Activity:	Solution:
2 **r** en las **p**	2 **rodillas** en las **piernas**
206 **h** en el **c**	206 **huesos** en el **cuerpo**
32 **d** en la **b**	32 **dientes** en la **boca**
1 **c** en el **p**	1 **corazón** en el **pecho**
10 **d d l p** en los **p**	10 **dedos de los pies** en los **pies**

El Calendario:

Activity:	Solution:
52 **s** en un **a**	52 **semanas** en un **año**
7 **d** en una **s**	7 **días** en una **semana**
12 **m** en un **a**	12 **meses** en un **año**
30 **d** en **s, a, j** y **n**	30 **días** en **septiembre, abril, junio** y **noviembre**
28 **d** en **f**, 29 en **a b**	28 **días** en **febrero**, 29 en **año bisiesto**

Nuestra Clase:

Create sentences based on your own classroom. Fill in the numbers in the following sentences based on your classroom. You can use this activity to reinforce classroom words and encourage students to become better acquainted with their classroom environment. Possible sentences might include:

Activity:	Solution:
c en la **p**	**carteles** en la **pared**
e en la **c**	**estudiantes** en la **clase**
l en el **e**	**libros** en el **estante**
c en la **m**	**computadoras** en la **mesa**
c d a en el **e** del (de la) profesor(a)	**carpetas de argollas** en el **escritorio** del (de la) profesor(a)
c en el **l**	**capítulos** en el **libro**

Standards Targeted: 1.1, 1.2, and 1.3

36. Algo en común I

<table>
<tr><td>

Versión 1:

Las cosas en los siguientes grupos tienen algo en común. Tienes que averiguar qué tienen en común.

ejemplo: hambre • miedo • 15 años • razón

respuesta: cosas que tienes (todas estas palabras pueden ser parte de una expresión con el verbo tener)

1. el esposo de tu madre • una verdura • el líder de la iglesia católica

2. fotos • la basura • la tarea • notas

3. un gato • una película nueva • coca

</td><td>

Versión 2:

The items in each of the following sets share something in common. You have to find out what they have in common.

ejemplo: hambre • miedo • 15 años • razón

answer: cosas que tienes (all of these words can be used in "tener" expressions)

1. el esposo de tu madre • una verdura • el líder de la iglesia católica

2. fotos • la basura • la tarea • buenas notas

3. un gato • una película nueva • coca

</td></tr>
</table>

Presentation Suggestion:

If students are having a difficult time finding the solution, encourage them to write down their ideas. They can write out all of their ideas for each word and then see if there are any commonalities in the groups. Sometimes students expect to just "see" the answer, but this strategy can help them work toward the answer if it doesn't come to them right away.

Solution:

1. papas:

    papá: el esposo de tu madre

    una papa: una verdura

    el papa: el líder de la iglesia católica

2. cosas que sacas

3. cosas con colas

Standards Targeted: 1.1, 1.2, and 1.3

37. Algo en común II

<table>
<tr><td>Versión 1:</td><td>Versión 2:</td></tr>
</table>

Versión 1:

Las cosas en los siguientes grupos tienen algo en común. Tienes que averiguar qué tienen en común.

ejemplo: hambre • miedo • 15 años • razón

respuesta: cosas que tienes (todas estas palabras pueden ser parte de una expresión con el verbo tener)

1. tortilla • churros • paella • gazpacho

2. Chihuahua • León • Toluca

3. azul • blanco • un sol

Versión 2:

The items in each of the following sets share something in common. You have to find out what they have in common.

ejemplo: hambre • miedo • 15 años • razón

answer: cosas que tienes (all of these words can be used in "tener" expressions)

1. tortilla • churros • paella • gazpacho

2. Chihuahua • León • Toluca

3. azul • blanco • un sol

Presentation Suggestion:

If students are having a difficult time finding the solution, encourage them to write down their ideas. They can write out all of their ideas for each word and then see if there are any commonalities in the groups. Sometimes students expect to just "see" the answer, but this strategy can help them work toward the answer if it doesn't come to them right away.

Hint:

If students need a little extra help, you can let them know that all of the answers are related to Spanish-speaking countries.

Solution:

1. comidas tradicionales de España

2. ciudades en México

3. la bandera de Argentina

Standards Targeted: 1.1, 1.2, 1.3, and 3.1

38. Algo en común III

Versión 1:	Versión 2:
Las cosas en los siguientes grupos tienen algo en común. Tienes que averiguar qué tienen en común.	The items in each of the following sets share something in common. You have to find out what they have in common.
ejemplo: hambre • miedo • 15 años • razón	**ejemplo:** hambre • miedo • 15 años • razón
respuesta: cosas que tienes (todas estas palabras pueden ser parte de una expresión con el verbo tener)	**answer: cosas que tienes** (all of these words can be used in "tener" expressions)
1. dormir • poder • costar	1. dormir • poder • costar
2. mapa • gorila • planeta • problema	2. mapa • gorila • planeta • problema
3. si • tu • mi • el • te	3. si • tu • mi • el • te
4. mano • foto • radio	4. mano • foto • radio

Presentation Suggestion:

If students are having a difficult time finding the solution, encourage them to write down their ideas. They can write out all of their ideas for each word and then see if there are any commonalities in the groups. Sometimes students expect to just "see" the answer, but this strategy can help them work toward the answer if it doesn't come to them right away.

Hint:

If students need a little extra help, you can let them know that all of the answers are related to words/rules that Spanish students complain about! (They are all exceptions to general rules.)

Solution:

1. verbs that stem-change from "o" to "ue" in the present tense

2. words that are masculine but end in "a"

3. one-syllable words that have a different meaning when you add an accent

4. words that are feminine but end in "o"

Standards Targeted: 1.1, 1.2, and 1.3

39. Algo en común IV

Versión 1:	Versión 2:
Vas a crear grupos con palabras relacionadas. Vas a escribir una lista de palabras pero no escribas como están conectadas. Intenta hacer por lo menos dos grupos. **ejemplo:** hambre • miedo • 15 años • razón **respuesta: cosas que tienes** (todas estas palabras pueden ser parte de una expresión con el verbo tener) Cuando terminas, vas a cambiar papeles con otra persona. Tienes que averiguar la conexión en los grupos que tu pareja hizo.	You are going to create sets of related objects. You will list the words but not the relationship. Try to create at least two sets. **ejemplo:** hambre • miedo • 15 años • razón **answer: cosas que tienes** (all of these words can be used in "tener" expressions) Then you will trade papers with a partner. You will try to figure out the relationships in the sets your partner created.

Presentation Suggestion:

You may want to present this activity after students have done exercises 35 to 38 and have experience with this type of word puzzle.

This also works well as a whole-class activity. Students spend a few minutes trying to think of a group of related words. If they think of one, they can write it on the board. Students try to solve the problems on the board or continue adding new ones. After a set amount of time (usually three to five minutes), everyone stops and goes over all the problems and their solutions.

You can use this type of activity after each chapter. Think of words or topics from the chapter that are connected (sometimes in complicated ways). Present the words to students and see if they can find the connections. Engage students in a conversation about how the words are connected. This can be an excellent way to promote Spanish discussion and review the important chapter vocabulary or topics.

Standards Targeted: 1.1, 1.2, and 1.3

40. Mis parientes

Versión 1:	Versión 2:
Lee las siguientes descripciones sobre miembros de tu familia. Necesitas escribir el título (abuelo, tía, primo) correcto para la persona en la descripción.	Read the following descriptions about family members. You need to write the correct title (grandfather, uncle, cousin) for the person in the description.
Ejemplo:	Ejemplo:
la madre de tu madre = *abuela*	la madre de tu madre = *abuela*
1. la hija de mi padre	1. la hija de mi padre
2. la abuela de mi hermana	2. la abuela de mi hermana
3. el hijo del hermano de mi madre	3. el hijo del hermano de mi madre
4. la esposa de mi tío	4. la esposa de mi tío
5. la hija de mi madrastra	5. la hija de mi madrastra

Presentation Suggestion:

If students have a difficult time with this type of exercise suggest that they look at a family tree (or quickly draw a simple family tree). Then, they can trace the relationships in the questions and find the solution visually.

Solution:

1. la hija de mi padre = mi hermana

2. la abuela de mi hermana = mi abuela

3. el hijo del hermano de mi madre = mi primo

4. la esposa de mi tío = mi tía

5. la hija de mi madrastra = mi hermanastra

Variations and Additional Activities:

Ask students to create their own clues for family members. Then, have students exchange their clues and see if their partners can solve the clues.

Standards Targeted: 1.1, 1.2, and 1.3

41. Mi familia

Versión 1:	Versión 2:
Necesitas resolver los siguientes problemas.	Solve the following problems.

Versión 1:

Necesitas resolver los siguientes problemas.

1. Mi familia tiene 5 hijos y en total tienen 55 años. Yo soy la mayor y tengo 18 años. Silvia tiene 2 años menos que yo. Laura y Lola son gemelas. Marcos tiene 6 años más que Laura o Lola.

2. Mi familia tiene 5 personas: mi mamá, mi papá, mi hermana menor (Sara), mi hermano mayor (Juan) y yo. Mi papá tiene tres veces mi edad. Mi mamá tiene dos veces la edad de Juan. Juntos mis padres tienen 87 años. Sara tiene 13 años. En total mi familia tiene 136 años. ¿Cuántos años tiene cada persona en mi familia?

Versión 2:

Solve the following problems.

1. Mi familia tiene 5 hijos y en total tienen 55 años. Yo soy la mayor y tengo 18 años. Silvia tiene 2 años menos que yo. Laura y Lola son gemelas. Marcos tiene 6 años más que Laura o Lola.

2. Mi familia tiene 5 personas: mi mamá, mi papá, mi hermana menor (Sara), mi hermano mayor (Juan) y yo. Mi papá tiene tres veces mi edad. Mi mamá tiene dos veces la edad de Juan. Juntos mis padres tienen 87 años. Sara tiene 13 años. En total mi familia tiene 136 años. ¿Cuántos años tiene cada persona en mi familia?

Presentation Suggestion:

If time allows, ask students to share how they came to their solutions. This can be a nice opportunity to connect Spanish with other subject areas (mathematics). Some students may use trial and error, others may solve algebraically, and others may be able to solve the problem without writing out the steps. If you would like students to practice the verb "tener" with ages, ask them to write out their answers in complete sentences.

Variations and Additional Activities:

Consider creating other logic problems that feature the chapter vocabulary or other topics that you are studying. Students may also enjoy creating logic problems for their classmates. You can use this type of exercise with a wide variety of topics.

Solution:

1. Laura = 5 años
   Lola = 5 años
   Marcos = 11 años
   Silvia = 16 años
   Yo = 18 años

2. Mamá = 42 años
   Papá = 45 años
   Sara = 13 años
   Juan = 21 años
   Yo = 15 años

Standards Targeted: 1.1, 1.2, 1.3, and 3.1

Cultura

Activities that encourage students to
connect with other people and cultures

42. ¿Qué puede ser?

Preparation

The following exercises require students to look at a photograph and describe the object pictured and how it is used. Make photocopies of the pictures or display them on a projector. The pictures are all included on page 59.

Versión 1:	Versión 2:
Mira la foto. ¿Qué puede ser este objeto? ¿Para qué se usa? ¿De dónde es? Incluye muchos detalles sobre tus ideas.	Look at the following picture. What do you think the object is? What is it used for? Where is it from? Describe your theory in as much detail as possible.

Presentation Suggestion:

Three pictures are included on page 59. You can use one picture a day and use this activity for three days or include all of the pictures as a one-day activity.

You may need to remind students that all of the objects featured in these activities are school appropriate. Consequently, students should only provide theories that are also appropriate for school.

Encourage students to ask each other questions and discuss their theories in Spanish. The goal is to engage students in rich discussions. As a fun twist, you could also vote on which student had the most creative idea or which student had the most detailed and plausible answer.

Solution:

1. These objects are called a mate and bombilla. The gourd is called a mate. Mates and bombillas are popular in many South American countries and this particular one came from Argentina. People put herbs (yerba) into the gourd and then fill the mate with water (usually hot water). Then, people drink through the bombilla. The bombilla is usually made of silver and has holes in the bottom that allow the tea through but block the herb pieces.

2. This object is a Mexican Molinillo. It is used to mix hot chocolate (much like a whisk). To use, you hold the handle between your hands and roll them back and forth quickly. By moving quickly, you can froth the hot chocolate.

3. This object is a traditional cafetera from Costa Rica. You would put the coffee grounds into the bag and pour water through the bag into a coffee cup. Although this is clearly a very simple coffee maker, it does serve its purpose. Now, many people use more elaborate cafeterias, and this item would not be as common.

Variations and Additional Activities:

Bring in an interesting item to feature for this exercise. If you cannot bring in the actual item, find a photograph. When possible, select an item that relates to what you are currently studying. Allow students to pass around the object and examine it carefully.

Sample Items: There are a variety of interesting musical instruments (such as castañuelas, flutes, or maracas) that would fit well with this type of exercise. You could use a paellera from Spain if studying food. A peineta or mantilla from a Flamenco dancer could fit well with a unit on clothing. Consider developing a small collection of interesting items that you can use for this type of activity.

Also ask students to bring in interesting items they may have from other countries. Students could share items from Spanish-speaking countries or other places around the world. If students go on vacations to Spanish-speaking countries, request that they bring back photographs or items that can be used for this type of activity. Encourage students to share what they learned about these items during their travel abroad.

Standards Targeted: 1.1, 1.2, 1.3, 2.1, 2.3, and 4.2

¿Qué Puede Ser?

1.

2.

3.

43. Mis experiencias

Versión 1:	Versión 2:
¿Has visitado algún país hispanohablante? ¿Conoces a alguien que es de un país hispanohablante? ¿Alguna vez has necesitado usar el español en tu vida diaria? Describe tus experiencias con el español y con los países hispanohablantes.	Have you ever traveled to a Spanish-speaking country? Do you know someone from a Spanish-speaking country? Have you ever needed to use Spanish in your life? Please describe your experiences with Spanish and Spanish-speaking countries.
Si no tienes ninguna experiencia para describir, escribe sobre qué país te gustaría visitar y por qué.	If you don't have any experiences to describe, tell us what Spanish-speaking country you would like to visit and why.

Solution:

Answers will vary. Encourage students to describe their experiences with the class. This exercise can be a good opportunity to remind students of the tremendous value in learning another language!

Variations and Additional Activities:

As a followup, ask students if they have any photographs from traveling to a Spanish-speaking country. Have students share their photographs with their classmates. Require students to find ways to use Spanish outside of the classroom and then have them report back to the class in a week or two. For example, students could read a magazine in Spanish, try to speak in Spanish with someone who is from another country, or watch TV in Spanish.

Standards Targeted: 1.1, 1.2, 1.3, 5.1, and 5.2

44. 21 Países

Versión 1:	Versión 2:
Hay 21 países donde hablan español (y también es una lengua oficial). Intenta hacer una lista de los 21 países hispano-hablantes.	There are 21 countries where Spanish is spoken (and it is also an official language). Try to create a list of the 21 Spanish-speaking countries.

Presentation Suggestion:

If students don't know all of the countries, encourage them to use a map and try to hypothesize which countries speak Spanish. This will also help students learn where the countries are located and to make intelligent guesses based on their knowledge of geography and world history.

Note: If you are going to do exercise #45 tomorrow or in the near future, you may want students to keep their lists after you go over them so they can add the capitals.

Solution:

1. Argentina
2. Bolivia
3. Chile
4. Colombia
5. Costa Rica
6. Cuba
7. Ecuador
8. España
9. Guatemala
10. Honduras
11. Guinea Equatorial
12. México
13. Nicaragua
14. Panamá
15. Paraguay
16. Perú
17. Puerto Rico
18. La República Dominicana
19. El Salvador
20. Uruguay
21. Venezuela

Standards Targeted: 1.1, 1.2, 1.3, and 3.1

45. Las capitales

Versión 1:
¿Sabes las capitales de los países hispano-hablantes? Intenta hacer una lista con los 21 países hispanohablantes y sus capitales.

Versión 2:
Do you know all the capitals for the Spanish-speaking countries? Try to make a list of the 21 Spanish-speaking countries with their capitals.

Presentation Suggestion:

If you do problem #44 the day before this one, ask students to keep their lists of countries after you go over them in class. Then students can simply add the capitals to it. If you think this will be too challenging for students, create a word bank on the board with all the capitals. Students can try to match the capitals with the countries. Or, allow students to use a map (which will also help students with their geography knowledge and skills).

Solution:

1. Argentina – Buenos Aires
2. Bolivia – La Paz
3. Chile – Santiago
4. Colombia – Bogotá
5. Costa Rica – San José
6. Cuba – La Habana
7. Ecuador – Quito
8. España (Spain) – Madrid
9. Guatemala – Guatemala
10. Honduras – Tegucigalpa
11. Guinea Equatorial – Malabo
12. México – México D.F.
13. Nicaragua – Managua
14. Panamá – Panamá
15. Paraguay – Asunción
16. Perú – Lima
17. Puerto Rico – San Juan
18. La República Dominicana – Santo Domingo
19. El Salvador – San Salvador
20. Uruguay – Montevideo
21. Venezuela – Caracas

Additional Information:

Sucre is the constitutional capital of Bolivia. It was the first capital and is the home of the Supreme Court. Consequently, some sources list Bolivia as having two capitals while others list only La Paz.

Variations and Additional Activities:

Write each capital and country on an index card. As students enter your room, give each an index card. Have the students find their matching countries or capitals and then sit down together. In addition to being a good warmup problem, this can be an interesting way to have students find partners for a class activity or project. If you want to do a group activity with three students, you could create index cards with various details about the country (such as the capital, currency, and flag).

Standards Targeted: 1.1, 1.2, 1.3, and 3.1

46. ¿Qué significan los nombres?

Versión 1:	Versión 2:
¿Qué significan los nombres de los países hispanohablantes? ¿Por qué se llaman…	What do the names of the Spanish-speaking countries mean? Why are they called…

♦ Costa Rica	♦ Costa Rica
♦ Ecuador	♦ Ecuador
♦ Bolivia	♦ Bolivia
♦ Puerto Rico	♦ Puerto Rico
♦ El Salvador	♦ El Salvador

Presentation Suggestion:

Students may wish to hypothesize how other countries got their names. Encourage students to investigate how other places were named.

Solution:

Costa Rica means rich or precious coast

Ecuador means equator; the country is located on the equator

Bolivia was named after Simon Bolívar who fought to liberate the South American countries from Spain

Puerto Rico means rich or precious port

El Salvador means the savior

Standards Targeted: 1.1, 1.2, 1.3, 3.1, and 3.2

47. Un nombre apropiado

Versión 1:	Versión 2:
Muchas veces, los países tienen nombres basados en alguna característica importante o un evento de la historia del país. Piensa en un lugar que has visitado. ¿Qué nombre sería un nombre apropiado para ese lugar? ¿Por qué?	Countries are often named based on a distinguishing characteristic or some part of the country's history. Think of a place you have visited. If you were going to rename that place, what would you call it? Why?

Presentation Suggestion:

This exercise is a good followup to #46. If students are taking a long time thinking of a place to name, encourage them to rename their hometown or state.

Standards Targeted: 1.1, 1.2, 1.3, and 3.1

48. Dinero extranjero

Versión 1:

Casi todos los países tienen dinero diferente. Intenta emparejar los países de la lista con su tipo de dinero:

País	Dinero
Bolivia	Colón
Costa Rica	Guaraní
España	Quetzal
Guatemala	Peso
México	Boliviano
Paraguay	Bolívar
Perú	Nuevo sol
Venezuela	Euro

Versión 2:

Almost every country has a different currency. Try to match the countries from the list below with their currencies:

País	Dinero
Bolivia	Colón
Costa Rica	Guaraní
España	Quetzal
Guatemala	Peso
México	Boliviano
Paraguay	Bolívar
Perú	Nuevo sol
Venezuela	Euro

Presentation Suggestion:

Many Spanish-speaking countries use pesos as their currency. However, it is important for students to note that they are not the same pesos. Remind students that in Canada their currency is called "dollars" but is different from the "dollars" used in the United States. To avoid confusion, you may wish to present a limited number of currencies (as listed above). However, you may also wish to go ahead and present all twenty-one countries' currencies.

If possible, bring samples of the different currencies to show your students. Many samples are available on the Internet and they can be printed for your students to look at.

Solution:

(The following list includes all of the currencies and not just the eight featured in the problem.)

1. Bolivia   Boliviano
2. España (Spain)   Euro
3. Guatemala   Quetzal
4. México   Peso
5. Paraguay   Guaraní
6. Perú   Nuevo sol
7. Venezuela   Bolívar

Standards Targeted: 1.1, 1.2, 1.3, and 3.1

49. Las escuelas

Versión 1:

Lee el siguiente párrafo sobre la escuela de Pedro en España.

¡Hola! Me llamo Pedro y tengo 13 años. Vivo en Madrid. Todos los días camino a mi escuela. La escuela empieza a las nueve y media. A la una tenemos la hora del almuerzo. Regreso a casa y como con mi mamá y mis tres hermanitas. A las dos regreso a la escuela. Las clases terminan a las cuatro y media. Después de las clases practico fútbol con mi equipo. Llego a mi casa a las 6 y media o a las siete.

Me gustan algunas de mis clases. Este semestre saqué un 9 en inglés y literatura. Son mis clases favoritas. Tengo ochos en muchas de mis clases. No me gusta mucho la clase de matemáticas. Tengo un 7 en esa clase. Debo estudiar más.

¿Cómo son similares o diferentes la escuela de Pedro y tu escuela?

Versión 2:

Read the following paragraphs about schools in Spain.

¡Hola! Me llamo Pedro y tengo 13 años. Vivo en Madrid. Todos los días camino a mi escuela. La escuela empieza a las nueve y media. A la una tenemos la hora del almuerzo. Regreso a casa y como con mi mamá y mis tres hermanitas. A las dos regreso a la escuela. Las clases terminan a las cuatro y media. Después de las clases practico fútbol con mi equipo. Llego a mi casa a las 6 y media o a las siete.

Me gustan algunas de mis clases. Este semestre saqué un 9 en inglés y literatura. Son mis clases favoritas. Tengo ochos en muchas de mis clases. No me gusta mucho la clase de matemáticas. Tengo un 7 en esa clase. Debo estudiar más.

How is Pedro's school in Madrid similar to or different from your school?

Presentation Suggestion:

Modify the selection to meet your students' needs and your curricular goals.

Solution:

Answers will vary. Encourage students to engage in meaningful discussions with their classmates. Students may note that the school day begins later than most American schools. Many Spanish students still go home for their lunch break. However, this practice is beginning to change for a variety of reasons. In Spain, and many other Spanish-speaking countries, students earn numerical grades from one to ten instead of letter grades.

Standards Targeted: 1.1, 1.2, 1.3, 2.1, 3.1, 3.2, and 4.2

50. Nombres completos

Versión 1:	Versión 2:
En España, la gente generalmente usa dos apellidos. Los españoles usan su apellido paterno seguido por su apellido materno.	In Spain, people generally use two surnames (last names). Generally, people use their father's surname followed by their mother's.
Ejemplo: **Susana Pérez González**	Example: **Susana Pérez González**
Pérez es el apellido paterno de Susana. González es el apellido materno de Susana.	Pérez would be Susana's paternal surname. González would be Susana's maternal surname.
Ahora, muchos hispanos que viven en los Estados Unidos usan un guión entre sus dos apellidos porque los americanos que no conocen esta tradición piensan que el apellido paterno es un segundo nombre (middle name).	Hispanics who live in the United States sometimes hyphenate their last names because people who aren't familiar with this custom mistake the paternal surname for a middle name.
¿Qué sería tu nombre completo en España? ¿Cuáles son algunas ventajas o desventajas de esta tradición?	What would your full name be in Spain? Can you see any advantages or disadvantages to this custom?

Presentation Suggestion:

If you have students who live with single parents or who are adopted, they may not want to discuss their full names (or may not know what their full names would be). In this case, you could provide family trees for celebrities or fictitious people so that students could identify full names without discussing their own private family situations. Also, some students might like to know that in Spain, single mothers sometimes use their own last names twice. In the example, the girl's name would be Susana González González.

Additional Information:

Although this exercise focuses on Spain, these naming traditions apply to most Spanish-speaking countries.

Standards Targeted: 1.1, 1.2, 1.3, 2.1, and 4.2

51. Nombres y el matrimonio

Preparation

Provide students with a copy of the "Nombres y el matrimonio" handout or display the information on the board or projector. Versión 1 and Versión 2 are included on the next page. The handout provides students with information about naming practices in Spanish-speaking countries and then asks the students to articulate their thoughts about these practices.

Presentation Suggestion:

Because this exercise builds on the information students learned in #49, you may want to do this exercise the day after #49.

Variations and Additional Activities:

To practice this naming practice, you could do an activity with celebrity marriages. Ask students to imagine two celebrities getting married (you will need to invent maternal names). Then, have the students pick names for the celebrities' children. Students can be very interested in naming the imaginary children of their favorite celebrities.

As a followup activity, encourage students to research naming practices in other countries. Ask students to share this information with the class.

Standards Targeted: 1.1, 1.2, 1.3, 2.1, and 4.2

Nombres y el matrimonio (versión 1)

Como ya sabes, los españoles usan dos apellidos (paterno y materno).

Ejemplo: **Susana Pérez González**

Pérez es el apellido paterno de Susana. González es el apellido materno de Susana.

Cuando una mujer se casa, generalmente no cambia su nombre legal. A veces, la mujer deja de usar su apellido materno y en vez usa el apellido paterno de su esposo.

Ejemplo: Susana Pérez González se casa con Juan García Ramos

Susana puede usar el nombre:
Susana Pérez González (sin cambio)
Susana Pérez García o
Susana Pérez de García

Si Susana y Juan tienen un hijo que se llama Pablo su nombre completo sería Pablo Pérez García o Pablo García Pérez. Es más común usar el apellido paterno primero pero la ley dice que también se puede usar el apellido materno primero.

¿Qué piensas de esta tradición? ¿Cuáles son algunas ventajas de esta tradición?

Nombres y el matrimonio (versión 2)

As you know, in Spain, people generally use both their paternal and maternal surname.

Example: **Susana Pérez González**

Pérez would be Susana's paternal surname. González would be Susana's maternal surname.

When a woman gets married, she generally does *not* change her legal name. However, sometimes women will stop using their maternal surname and add their husband's paternal surname.

Example: Susana Pérez González married Juan García Ramos

Susana *could* use:
Susana Pérez González (no change)
Susana Pérez García or
Susana Pérez de García

If they had a son named "Pablo" his name would be either:
Pablo Pérez García *or*
Pablo García Pérez

It is more common for the paternal name to come first but either is legally acceptable.

What do you think of this custom? What are some benefits to this system?

52. Los uniformes

Versión 1:	Versión 2:
En muchos países hispanohablantes, los estudiantes tienen que llevar uniformes en las escuelas. ¿Por qué crees que llevan uniformes? ¿Te gustan los uniformes? ¿Por qué te gustan o por qué no te gustan?	In many Spanish-speaking countries, students have to wear uniforms to school. Why do you think they have to wear uniforms? Do you like uniforms? Why or why not?

Presentation Suggestion:

If you have access to some, show your students pictures of students in other countries wearing uniforms.

Variations and Additional Activities:

Divide the class in half and require that half of them argue in favor of uniforms and the other half argue against uniforms.

As a followup activity, have students design and describe a uniform for your school. Encourage students to be creative.

Solution:

Students' opinions will vary. Encourage students to think about the many uses or benefits and the drawbacks of uniforms. For example, uniforms can equalize students by deemphasizing expensive, fashionable clothes. Uniforms also help teachers and administrators make sure students are dressed appropriately without getting into specific fashion trends. Some teachers believe uniforms help students express their individuality as people, instead of their individuality through expensive means such as clothing. However, some people believe that uniforms don't give students sufficient opportunity to express their individual styles.

Additional information:

In some countries, such as Venezuela, students' uniforms are color-coded. Daycare-age children wear yellow tops, kindergarten and preschool wear red, elementary wear white, middle school and lower high school wear blue, and upper high school wear tan. All students must wear dark blue skirts or pants. Each school puts their emblem on the shirts. This way teachers, school officials, and city officials can readily tell what age a student is and what school they attend. Some countries have national or citywide laws regarding uniforms.

As an extension to this problem, encourage students to investigate the constitutionality of uniforms in America. Students may be very interested in learning about their rights as Americans in terms of free speech and dress codes. Encourage students to share their findings.

Standards Targeted: 1.1, 1.2, 1.3, 2.1, 3.1, 3.2, and 4.2

53. Las siestas

Versión 1:	Versión 2:
En muchos países hispanohablantes, y en particular en España, la gente toma siestas al mediodía. ¿Por qué crees que toman siestas? ¿Te gustan las siestas?	In many Spanish-speaking countries, and in particular in Spain, people take "siestas" (naps) at midday. Why do you think they take naps? Do you like naps?

Solution:

Students' opinions will vary. Students may not realize that naps serve practical purposes, in addition to the value of rest. Because very few places in Spain are air-conditioned, the midday heat can be unbearable. Taking a nap in the afternoon can help people cope with the heat (especially in southern Spain), and then they can work more productively during cooler hours.

Additional Information:

Even today in Spain, "siestas" are relatively common. Many businesses (especially small or family-run businesses) shut down for a couple of hours in the middle of the day. People eat their big meal and then take a "siesta." Many schools still provide a long lunch break so students can walk home, eat a large lunch, and rest before returning to classes.

Standards Targeted: 1.1, 1.2, 1.3, 2.1, and 4.2

54. Palabras regionales

Versión 1:	Versión 2:
En algunas partes del mundo las personas tienen diferentes palabras para la misma cosa. Por ejemplo, en los Estados Unidos dicen "elevator" pero en Inglaterra dicen "lift." Mira la lista de palabras en inglés. Escoge las palabras del banco que tienen el mismo significado.	In some parts of the world people have different words that mean the same thing. For example, in the United States people say "elevator" but in England people say "lift." Look at the following list of English words. Then, choose the words from the bank that have the same meaning.

Banco de palabras:

mantequilla	torta
ascensor	albaricoque
autobús	bizcocho
queque	manteca
damasco	camión
pastel	elevador
guagua	

1. Cake
2. Bus
3. Elevator
4. Butter
5. Apricot

Banco de palabras:

mantequilla	torta
ascensor	albaricoque
autobús	bizcocho
queque	manteca
damasco	camión
pastel	elevador
guagua	

1. Cake
2. Bus
3. Elevator
4. Butter
5. Apricot

Presentation Suggestion:

If you have heritage speakers, encourage them to share which words they use or ask if they have additional words to add. Let students know that when they travel, it is important to learn what regional words are used. In some cases, a word that is used in one region may have a different meaning or connotation in another place. Remind students, however, that none of the words is wrong; each word is just a different regional variation. When appropriate add words from your chapter vocabulary to the activity.

Solution:

1. Cake: torta, bizcocho, pastel, queque

2. Bus: guagua, autobús, camión

3. Elevator: elevador, ascensor

4. Butter: mantequilla, manteca

5. Apricot: albaricoque, damasco

Standards Targeted: 1.1, 1.2, 1.3, 2.1, and 4.1

55. Palabras regionales II

Versión 1:	**Versión 2:**
En algunas partes del mundo, las personas tienen diferentes palabras para la misma cosa. Por ejemplo, en los Estados Unidos, dicen "elevator," pero en Inglaterra, dicen "lift." Mira la lista de palabras en inglés. Escoge las palabras del banco que tienen el mismo significado.	In some parts of the world, people have different words that mean the same thing. For example, in the United States, people say "elevator," but in England, people say "lift." Look at the following list of English words. Then, try to choose the words from the bank that have the same meaning.

Versión 1:

Banco de palabras:

anteojos	*césped*
aguacate	*carro*
gafas	*palta*
lentes	*pasto*
rositas de maíz	*coche*
prado	*cotufas*
espejuelos	*automóvil*
hierba (yerba)	*palomitas de maíz*

1. Avocado
2. Glasses
3. Grass/Lawn
4. Popcorn
5. Car

Versión 2:

Banco de palabras:

anteojos	*césped*
aguacate	*carro*
gafas	*palta*
lentes	*pasto*
rositas de maíz	*coche*
prado	*cotufas*
espejuelos	*automóvil*
hierba (yerba)	*palomitas de maíz*

1. Avocado
2. Glasses
3. Grass/Lawn
4. Popcorn
5. Car

Presentation Suggestion:

This activity can be used as a followup to #54 or independently. When appropriate, add words from your chapter vocabulary to the activity.

Solution:

1. Avocado: aguacate, palta

2. Glasses: anteojos, gafas, lentes, espejuelos

3. Grass/Lawn: césped, pasto, prado, hierba (yerba)

4. Popcorn: rositas de maíz, cotufas, palomitas de maíz

5. Car: carro, coche, automóvil

Standards Targeted: 1.1, 1.2, 1.3, 2.1, and 4.1

56. ¿Qué dicen los animales?

Versión 1:	Versión 2:
En diferentes idiomas, hay diferentes maneras de representar como hablan los animales. Mira la lista siguiente y empareja los animales con el sonido (en español) que hacen.	In different languages, there are different ways of representing how animals talk. Look at the following list and match the animals with the sound they make (in Spanish).

Animal:	Sonido:	Animal:	Sonido:
Burro	Meee	Burro	Meee
Caballo	Ji-jo	Caballo	Ji-jo
Gallo	Gaua	Gallo	Gaua
Lobo	Goro goro goro	Lobo	Goro goro goro
Oveja	Auuh	Oveja	Auuh
Pájaro	Pío pío	Pájaro	Pío pío
Pavo	Qui-qui-ri-quí	Pavo	Qui-qui-ri-quí
Perro	Beee	Perro	Beee
Vaca	Ihiii	Vaca	Ihiii

Presentation Suggestion:

This can be a noisy problem for students to work through! If students read the words thinking of the way letters sound in English, they will struggle identifying the correct animals. However, by sounding the words out using correct Spanish pronunciation, they should be able to identify the animals. Many students may need to actually make the sounds out loud (plus they will enjoy it!).

If you have students in your class who speak other languages, encourage them to share how animal sounds are represented in their language. Also, you may want students to think of alternate ways of representing animal sounds that they believe are more accurate.

Solution:

Burro (donkey): Ji-jo
Caballo (horse): Ihiii
Gallo (rooster): Qui-qui-ri-quí
Lobo (wolf): Auuh
Oveja (sheep): Beee
Pájaro (bird): Pío pío
Pavo (turkey): Goro goro goro
Perro (dog): Gaua
Vaca (cow): Meee

Standards Targeted: 1.1, 1.2, 1.3, and 4.1

57. La jerga de España

Versión 1:	Versión 2:

Versión 1:

La mayoría de la gente usa la jerga (slang) de vez en cuando. Las siguientes palabras vienen de España. Intenta emparejar las palabras con sus descripciones.

Boli	Profe	Pelas
Majo(a)	Guay	Tertulia
Vale	Tío(a)	Móvil

Mala pata

1. un teléfono celular
2. algo muy bueno (en inglés "cool")
3. un bolígrafo
4. mala suerte
5. está bien (en inglés "ok")
6. dinero
7. un profesor
8. un chico/un chica
9. alguien que es atractivo o muy amable
10. una conversación (generalmente una conversación informal)

Versión 2:

Most people use slang words at least some of the time. The following slang terms are used in Spain. See if you can match the words with their English meanings.

Boli	Profe	Pelas
Majo(a)	Guay	Tertulia
Vale	Tío(a)	Móvil

Mala pata

1. a cell phone
2. cool or really good
3. a pen
4. bad luck
5. ok/alright
6. money
7. teacher
8. guy/dude or girl
9. someone who is attractive; also used for someone who is really nice
10. chit-chat or informal conversation (often over coffee)

Presentation Suggestion:

Please remind students that these terms are used in Spain. Slang varies tremendously in different countries, regions, and cities. It is important for students to recognize that some words can have different meanings in other locations. If you have heritage speakers, you may want to encourage them to share some school-appropriate slang with the class.

Variations and Additional Activities:

Encourage students to find additional school-appropriate slang. Ask the students to share the words in class as the following warmup problem. You could also create a bulletin board featuring your class slang.

Solution:

1. móvil	4. mala pata	7. profe	10. tertulia
2. guay	5. vale	8. tío(a)	
3. boli	6. pelas	9. majo(a)	

Standards Targeted: 1.1, 1.2, 1.3, and 4.1

Fechas importantes

Activities that relate to holidays and celebrations
from Spanish-speaking countries

58. El 16 de septiembre

Preparation:

Copy the appropriate student handout (either versión 1 or versión 2). The student handouts are found on the next page.

Presentation Suggestion:

Have students read the appropriate handout individually or with a partner.

After students have enough time to read the selection, ask them to discuss it with a partners. Were they surprised to learn that Mexican Independence is celebrated on September 16 and not on May 5?

Consider providing students with some reading comprehension questions such as:

♦ On what day do Mexicans celebrate their independence?

¿Cuándo celebran los mexicanos su independencia?

♦ What is the "Grito de Dolores?"

¿Qué es el grito de dolores?

♦ How long did Mexicans fight for their independence from Spain?

¿Por cuántos años lucharon los mexicanos para su independencia?

♦ What does the president of Mexico do every year to reenact this event?

¿Qué hace el presidente de México cada año para recrear este evento?

Depending on your students' Spanish skills, engage them in a discussion about the holiday.

You may also be able to find a video of the annual celebration on TV or on the Internet. After students have read the selection, you could show a short video clip and then ask students about what the reenactment includes.

Standards Targeted: 1.1, 1.2, 1.3, 2.1, 3.1, and 3.2

El 16 de septiembre (versión 1)

¿Cuándo celebran los mexicanos su independencia? La celebración es el 16 de septiembre y no el cinco de mayo como piensan muchos americanos. En la noche del 15 de septiembre de 1810, el padre Hidalgo sonó las campanas de la iglesia llamando a la gente a luchar para su libertad. El padre Hidalgo también dio su famoso "Grito de dolores." La lucha contra los españoles empezó el 16 de septiembre.

Después de once años de guerra, España reconoció la independencia de México firmando el Tratado de Córdoba el 27 de septiembre de 1821.

Cada año, a las once de la noche, el presidente de México suena las campanas del Palacio Nacional en la ciudad de México. El presidente también repite "El grito de dolores" del balcón. Mucha gente va a la plaza para escuchar el grito y también pueden verlo en la televisión. El próximo día hay un desfile y otros eventos.

El presidente grita, "¡Viva México! ¡Viva la independencia. ¡Vivan los héroes!"

El 16 de septiembre (versión 2)

Do you know when Mexicans celebrate independence day? It is the 16th of September, not "el Cinco de Mayo" like some Americans believe. During the evening of September 15, 1810, Father Hidalgo rang church bells calling his people to fight for freedom. Father Hidalgo also gave the famous "Grito de Dolores" (literally "Cry from Dolores"). Fighting against Spanish forces began on September 16.

On September 27, 1821, after eleven years of fighting, Mexico's independence was recognized under the Treaty of Córdoba.

Every year the president of Mexico rings the bells at 11 PM in the National Palace in Mexico City. He also repeats the "Grito de Dolores" from the balcony. Many people crowd the plaza and watch the event on television. The following day includes a parade and other festivities.

The president usually shouts, "¡Viva México! ¡Viva la Independencia. ¡Vivan los héroes!"

59. La influencia de Colón

Versión 1:	Versión 2:
Probablemente sabes que Colón y sus tres barcos llegaron a las Américas en 1492. Su viaje empezó una época de exploración y colonización de las Américas.	As you probably know, in 1492 Columbus sailed the ocean blue and arrived in the Americas. His trip led to many Europeans also exploring and colonizing the Americas.
Colón era un marinero italiano, pero la monarquía española pagó por su viaje. Si Fernando e Isabela (los reyes españoles) no hubieran pagado por el viaje, ¿cómo sería diferente nuestro mundo? ¿Cómo sería diferente el mundo si otro país hubiera pagado por el viaje?	Columbus was an Italian sailor; however, the Spanish monarchy funded his voyage. How would the Americas be different if Ferdinand and Isabel (the Spanish king and queen) had *not* been willing to fund his voyage? What if another country, such as Italy, had provided the ships and supplies? How do you think Columbus' voyage impacts our life *today*?
¿Cómo tiene el viaje de Colón una influencia en tu vida diaria?	

Presentation Suggestion:

Students may initially think that Columbus' voyage had no impact on their lives. Encourage them to probe the topic in greater depth. They may need to converse with partners to help think through their ideas. Also, you may want to ask students to share additional background information about Columbus or his voyages.

Solution:

Answers will vary. Some topics for students to consider:

♦ If another country had made claims to the Americas, what language would be predominant? Which country do you think would have been likely to encounter the Americas?

♦ If Europeans had come later and the Aztecs and Incas were more powerful, could they possibly have avoided being conquered? How would that change our world?

♦ How would "traditional" dishes in Europe and around the world be different without the "Columbian Exchange?" What other items, aside from food, were exchanged between the "new world" and the "old world?"

Standards Targeted: 1.1, 1.2, 1.3, 2.1, 2.2, 3.1, 3.2, 4.1, and 4.2

60. El día de los muertos

Preparation

Copy the following crossword puzzle for students. Two versions are presented on pages 80 and 81; select the one that is most appropriate for your students.

Solution:

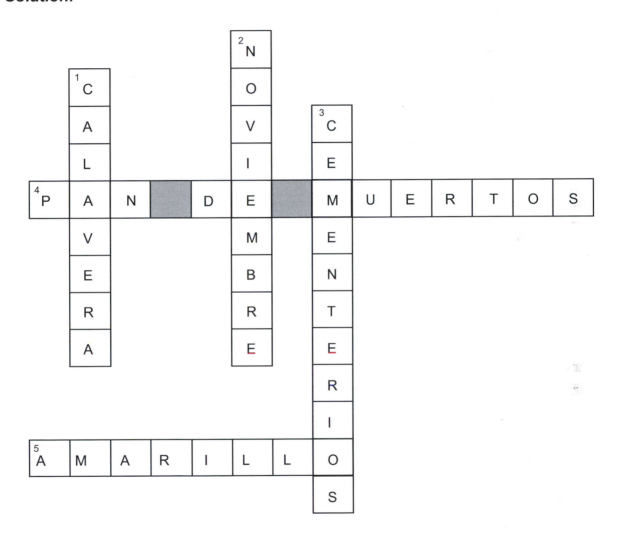

Standards Targeted: 1.1, 1.2, 1.3, and 2.1

El día de los muertos (versión 1)

Usa las siguientes pistas para completar el crucigrama.

1. Un dulce especial es una _____ hecha de azúcar.

2. Los mexicanos toman dos días para recordar a las personas queridas que ya están muertas. Estos días son el 1 y 2 de _____.

3. Las familias van a los _____ y ponen decoraciones. A veces también comen un picnic allí.

4. Otra comida típica es _____.

5. Las flores que usan para decorar típicamente son de color_____.

El día de los muertos (versión 2)

Answer the following clues in Spanish to complete the crossword puzzle.

1. A special treat for day of the dead is a _____ or a sugar skull.

2. This holiday is a time for Mexicans to remember special people who have passed away. The celebration takes place on the first and second of _____.

3. Families go to _____ to clean up and decorate. Sometimes they also have a picnic.

4. _____ or bread of the dead is another typical food.

5. People use marigolds to decorate for El Día de los muertos. What color are marigolds usually?

61. Dando gracias

Versión 1:	Versión 2:
El día de acción de gracias es un día festivo en los Estados Unidos. Muchos latinos que viven en los Estados Unidos ahora celebran este día. Para muchos es una oportunidad para pensar en las muchas cosas que tenemos y dar gracias. ¿Cuáles son algunas de las cosas qué tienes qué te gustan? ¿Por cuáles cosas das gracias?	Thanksgiving is an American holiday. Many Latinos who live in the United States have begun celebrating this day. For many people, this is an opportunity to think about the many things that we have and to give thanks. What are some of the things that you have that you appreciate? What are you thankful for?

Presentation Suggestion:

In addition to having students think about what they are thankful for, students could create simple cards to thank others. Consider providing students with some sample phrases they could use on the front of the cards and then have students write a personalized note inside the card.

Standards Targeted: 1.1, 1.2, 1.3, and 2.1

62. Metas para el año nuevo

Versión 1:	Versión 2:
Cada año muchas personas piensan en metas para el año nuevo. Pensar en metas puede ayudarte a trabajar en diferentes cosas. Escribe cinco metas para el año nuevo.	Many people write goals or resolutions for the New Year. Thinking of goals can help you work on different aspects of your life. Try to write five goals for the New Year.
	Ejemplo:
	Este año voy a terminar mi tarea antes de las 11 de la noche.

Presentation Suggestion:

Consider providing your students with multiple sample sentences so they can see how to structure their responses. Encourage students to discuss their goals with each other and the whole class.

Standards Targeted: 1.1, 1.2, and 1.3

63. Año nuevo

Versión 1:	Versión 2:
En diferentes países tienen diferentes maneras de celebrar el año nuevo y la víspera del año nuevo. Por ejemplo, en España hay una tradición de comer 12 uvas. Todos esperan hasta la medianoche y las personas comen una uva cada vez que la campana suena. Hay fiestas grandes y las personas celebran en las plazas de las ciudades y los pueblos. ¿Cómo celebras el año nuevo? ¿Tiene tu familia una tradición especial?	In different countries, people have different ways of celebrating New Year's Day and New Year's Eve. For example, in Spain there is a tradition of eating 12 grapes. Everyone waits until midnight and then eats a grape each time the bell chimes. There are big parties and people gather to celebrate in the city or town's plaza. How do you celebrate the New Year? Does your family have a special tradition? Write as much in Spanish as possible.

Presentation Suggestion:

For students who need more assistance, consider providing them with a sample (such as your New Year's traditions). You could also provide them with some possible sentences that they could fill in (e.g., "En mi familia nosotros..." or "Para el Año Nuevo me gusta..."). Encourage students to write in as much detail as possible.

Variations and Additional Activities:

To turn this into a simple game, collect students' responses once they finish. Then, read the students' responses one at a time, and have others try to guess who wrote each response.

Ask students to research New Year's traditions in other countries. Have students share their findings as a future warm-up activity.

Standards Targeted: 1.1, 1.2, 1.3, and 2.1

64. El día de los Reyes Magos

Versión 1:

En España, generalmente la gente no recibe regalos el 25 de diciembre. Reciben regalos el 6 de enero. ¿Sabes por qué?

El 6 de enero es el día de los Reyes Magos. El 5 de enero hay una cabalgata de los reyes (parade) y los niños reciben muchos dulces.

Antes de dormirse el 5 de enero, los niños dejan sus zapatos en el balcón o cerca de una ventana. Los Reyes Magos vienen durante la noche y dejan dulces y regalos para los niños.

Responde a las siguientes preguntas.

1. ¿Qué hacen los niños la noche del 5 de enero? ¿Por qué?

2. ¿Qué es una cabalgata?

¿Has visto la cabalgata de los reyes en la televisión alguna vez?

Versión 2:

Read the following selection and try to answer the questions.

En España, generalmente la gente no recibe regalos el 25 de diciembre. Reciben regalos el 6 de enero. ¿Sabes por qué?

El 6 de enero es el día de los Reyes Magos. El 5 de enero hay una cabalgata de los reyes (parade) y los niños reciben muchos dulces.

Antes de dormirse el 5 de enero, los niños dejan sus zapatos en el balcón o cerca de una ventana. Los Reyes Magos vienen durante la noche y dejan dulces y regalos para los niños.

Answer the following questions.

1. What do children do the night of January 5? Why?

2. What is a "cabalgata?" Have you ever seen "La Cabalgata de los Reyes" on television?

Presentation Suggestion:

Modify the reading as appropriate to meet your students needs and interests. You also may want to focus on different aspects of the holiday, depending on how they align with your curricular goals.

Additional Information:

Like many Spanish holidays, this holiday has a Christian origin. "Los Reyes Magos," or the Three Kings, were said to have visited Jesus in Bethlehem after his birth. The Kings brought gifts to present to baby Jesus. Therefore, the celebration of Kings day includes a gift-exchange, although Christmas day traditionally does not. However, in modern-day Spain, many children now receive gifts on Christmas day and enjoy the tradition of Santa Claus bringing gifts. You may want to share this information with students to help them understand some of the traditional Spanish celebrations.

Solution:

1. Children leave their shoes out on the balcony or windows, if they don't have balconies. They do this so that the Three Kings can fill their shoes with candy and presents.

2. Answers will vary. Many American cities have a Kings Day parade. You may want to look into local celebrations or celebrations that are televised through Spanish-speaking stations.

Variations and Additional Activities:

If time permits, consider showing students pictures or a video of a "calbagata de los reyes." Many American cities with large Hispanic populations have these parades and they are broadcast on television or via the Internet.

Standards Targeted: 1.1, 1.2, 1.3, 2.1, 3.1, and 3.2

65. El día de los Inocentes

Versión 1:

En los países hispanohablantes se celebra el día de los inocentes el 28 de diciembre. Esta celebración es muy similar a "April Fool's Day" en los Estados Unidos. Muchas personas hacen bromas o trucos y muchos de los periódicos imprimen por lo menos una historia falsa.

¿Qué broma graciosa te gustaría hacer? Si no puedes pensar en una broma, ¿qué historia graciosa te gustaría imprimir en el periódico escolar?

Versión 2:

Spanish-speaking countries celebrate "El día de los inocentes" on December 28th. This holiday is very similar to April Fool's day in the United States. Many people play tricks on each other and newspapers often run at least one fake story.

What is a fun prank that you would like to play on someone? If you can't think of a prank, what is a fake story that would be funny to run in the school newspaper?

Additional Information:

This holiday has a religious origin. The full title of the day is "Día de los Santos Inocentes." This day commemorates all of the babies who were said to have been murdered because of King Herod's order around the time of Jesus' birth. King Herod was attempting to ensure that Jesus did not survive and therefore ordered that all baby boys be killed. Although this holiday is still recognized by the Catholic church for this reason, the religious aspect of the holiday has been forgotten by most people. Celebrations generally focus on fun-natured pranks without any religious meaning.

Standards Targeted: 1.1, 1.2, 1.3, and 2.1

66. Sanfermines

Versión 1:	Versión 2:
Los Sanfermines se celebran el 6 de julio en Pamplona, España. El festival incluye varios eventos, pero el más famoso es la corrida de los toros. Toros corren por las calles de la ciudad hasta llegar a la plaza de los toros. Los turistas y los españoles llenan las calles para correr con los toros. Obviamente es un evento muy peligroso y muchos han sido heridos, especialmente los que no siguen los consejos de seguridad.	On July 6, people in Pamplona, Spain, celebrate "Sanfermines." This festival has many elements, but the most famous is the running of the bulls. The town releases bulls that run through the city streets into the bull-fighting ring. Tourists and locals crowd the streets to run with the bulls. Clearly, the event is very dangerous and many people have been injured, especially those who do not follow safety tips.
¿Por qué participan tantas personas en este evento? ¿Cuáles con los beneficios y riesgos? ¿Te gustaría participar en la corrida?	Why do you think people want to participate in this event? What are the benefits or risks? Would you want to participate?

Presentation Suggestion:

If students have never heard of this event, they may find it difficult to imagine or picture. There are many pictures and videos available through websites, travel programs, and teacher resources. Consider sharing some of this information with students prior to having them respond to this prompt.

Variations and Additional Activities:

At the end of the running of the bulls, the bulls are usually killed in a traditional bullfight. Engage students in a debate about bullfighting. Prior to the debate, you may need to provide students with some background information about bullfighting or ask that students do some research.

Standards Targeted: 1.1, 1.2, 1.3, and 2.1

67. ¿Qué día es?

<table>
<tr><td colspan="2">Versión 1:</td><td colspan="2">Versión 2:</td></tr>
</table>

Versión 1:	Versión 2:
Empareja los siguientes días festivos con las fechas apropiadas.	Match the following holidays with the appropriate dates.

Versión 1:

Empareja los siguientes días festivos con las fechas apropiadas.

- Día de la Independencia: la gente celebra el famoso Grito de Hidalgo
- Día de los Muertos
- Día de los Reyes
- Batalla de Puebla
- Día de la Raza

Fechas:

> El 1 y 2 de noviembre
> El 12 de octubre
> El 16 de septiembre
> El 6 de enero
> El 5 de mayo

¿Qué más sabes sobre estas fechas importantes?

Versión 2:

Match the following holidays with the appropriate dates.

- Día de la Independencia: la gente celebra el famoso Grito de Hidalgo
- Día de los Muertos
- Día de los Reyes
- Batalla de Puebla
- Día de la Raza

Fechas:

> El 1 y 2 de noviembre
> El 12 de octubre
> El 16 de septiembre
> El 6 de enero
> El 5 de mayo

What else do you know about these holidays?

Presentation Suggestion:

Modify which holidays are presented to align with your curricular goals.

Additional Information:

This exercise focuses on holidays in Mexico. However, some of these holidays are also celebrated in other Spanish-speaking countries, such as "El Día de los Reyes" and "El Día de la Raza." You may need to remind students that holidays differ throughout the Spanish-speaking world.

Solution:

El 6 de enero:	Día de los Reyes
El 5 de mayo:	Batalla de Puebla (Many students erroneously believe that "El Cinco de Mayo" is Mexico's independence day. However, "El Cinco de Mayo" is celebrated more by Latinos in the United States than by Mexicans living in Mexico.)
El 16 de septiembre:	Día de la Independencia: la gente celebra el famoso "Grito" de Hidalgo
El 12 de octubre:	Día de la Raza
El 1 y 2 de noviembre:	Día de los Muertos

Standards Targeted: 1.1, 1.2, 1.3, 2.1, 3.1, and 3.2

Aprendemos de los errores

Exercises that explore common errors

68. Cognados Falsos I

Versión 1:	Versión 2:
Un cognado falso es una palabra que parece una palabra en otro idioma pero significa otra cosa. Por ejemplo la palabra española "asistir" parece la palabra "to assist" en inglés, pero en realidad significa "to attend." Por eso llamamos "asistir" un cognado falso. Mira la siguiente lista. Todas las palabras son cognados falsos. Intenta traducir las palabras al inglés. Después usa un diccionario para verificar tus traducciones. Si tienes una palabra incorrecta, busca la palabra inglesa incorrecta en una diccionario para ver como se dice en español.	A false cognate is a word that looks like a word in another language but actually means something else. For example, the Spanish word "asistir" looks like the English word "assist," but it actually means "to attend." Therefore, we call "asistir" a false cognate. Look at the following list. All of the words are false cognates. Try to translate the words into English. Then, use a dictionary to check your translations. If you have a word wrong, look up the incorrect English word to see how you would actually say that in Spanish.
1. carpeta	1. carpeta
2. éxito	2. éxito
3. vaso	3. vaso
4. sopa	4. sopa
5. recordar	5. recordar

Presentation Suggestion:

Modify this exercise to include false cognates that students already confuse or are likely to encounter in the near future in your curriculum. Consider displaying these (and other) false cognates on a bulletin board or wall in your classroom. Encourage students to refer to their lists of false cognates from time to time so they don't use these words incorrectly.

Solution:

Spanish:	Correct Translation:	Sometimes confused with:
1. carpeta	folder	carpet (la alfombra)
2. éxito	success	exit (la salida)
3. vaso	glass	vase (el jarrón)
4. sopa	soup	soap (el jabón)
5. recordar	to remember	record (grabar)

Standards Targeted: 1.1, 1.2, and 1.3

69. Cognados Falsos II

Versión 1:	Versión 2:
Un cognado falso es una palabra que parece una palabra en otro idioma pero significa otra cosa. Por ejemplo la palabra española "asistir" parece la palabra "to assist" en inglés, pero en realidad significa "to attend." Por eso llamamos "asistir" un cognado falso. Mira la siguiente lista. Todas las palabras son cognados falsos. Intenta traducir las palabras al inglés. Después usa un diccionario para verificar tus traducciones. Si tienes una palabra incorrecta, busca la palabra inglesa incorrecta en una diccionario para ver como se dice en español.	A false cognate is a word that looks like a word in another language but actually means something else. For example, the Spanish word "asistir" looks like the English word "assist," but it actually means "to attend." Therefore, we call "asistir" a false cognate. Look at the following list. All of the words are false cognates. Try to translate the words into English. Then, use a dictionary to check your translations. If you have a word wrong, look up the incorrect English word to see how you would actually say that in Spanish.
1. chocar	1. chocar
2. largo	2. largo
3. fábrica	3. fábrica
4. ganga	4. ganga
5. ropa	5. ropa

Presentation Suggestion:

Modify this exercise to include false cognates that students already confuse or are likely to encounter in the near future in your curriculum. Consider displaying these (and other) false cognates on a bulletin board or wall in your classroom. Encourage students to refer to their lists of false cognates from time to time so they don't use these words incorrectly.

Solution:

Spanish:	Correct Translation:	Sometimes confused with:
1. chocar	to crash	choke (sofocar)
2. largo	long	large (grande)
3. fábrica	factory	fabric (la tela)
4. ganga	bargain	gang (pandilla)
5. ropa	clothes	rope (la cuerda)

Standards Targeted: 1.1, 1.2, and 1.3

70. ¿Qué pasó? (Problems with Homophones)

Versión 1:	Versión 2:
Los siguientes cuentos muestran algún tipo de error en traducir del español al inglés o del inglés al español. Lee los cuentos y describe que pasó.	The following stories show some kind of error translating from Spanish to English or English to Spanish. Read the stories and identify what went wrong.
En el supermercado:	**En el supermercado:**
Un hombre va a un supermercado para comprar los ingredientes para una pizza. No puede encontrar todo lo que necesita. Cuando el hombre habla con una dependienta ella responde, "No tenemos eso aquí. La floristería está en la Calle Bolívar."	Un hombre va a un supermercado para comprar los ingredientes para una pizza. No puede encontrar todo lo que necesita. Cuando el hombre habla con una dependienta ella responde, "No tenemos eso aquí. La floristería está en la Calle Bolívar."
De visita:	**De visita:**
Una niña está en su clase de español hablando sobre sus vacaciones. Ella dice que va a ir a México y va a visitar a la hermana de su mamá. La profesora responde, "Hay muchos insectos aquí. ¿Por qué quieres ir a México para ver insectos?"	Una niña está en su clase de español hablando sobre sus vacaciones. Ella dice que va a ir a México y va a visitar a la hermana de su mamá. La profesora responde, "Hay muchos insectos aquí. ¿Por qué quieres ir a México para ver insectos?"

Presentation Suggestion:

Modify the stories to use your chapter vocabulary or homophones that you know your students struggle with. Encourage your students to create short stories like these that you can use for future exercises.

Solution:

♦ En el supermercado: The miscommunication between the customer and the salesperson comes from confusion over the English homophones of "flour" and "flower." The customer is looking for "flour" and not "flower."

♦ De visita: The student in this story must have looked up the word "ant" instead of "aunt." Therefore, instead of talking about visiting her Mom's family she was talking about visiting an insect!

These types of translation errors are common when people look up the wrong homophone in a Spanish–English dictionary.

Standards Targeted: 1.1, 1.2, 1.3, and 4.1

71. ¿Qué pasó? II (Problems with Idioms)

Versión 1:	Versión 2:
El siguiente cuento muestra que Jorge no entiende todo lo que pasa en su nueva escuela. Lee el cuento y explica por qué Jorge no entiende todo.	The following story shows that Jorge does not understand what is going on. Read the story and see if you can find out what Jorge misunderstood.
Jorge es un niño guatemalteco. Él viaja a los Estados Unidos con un programa de intercambio. Después de su primer día en la escuela llama a sus padres.	Jorge es un niño guatemalteco. Él viaja a los Estados Unidos con un programa de intercambio. Después de su primer día en la escuela llama a sus padres.
Jorge: ¡Hola!	Jorge: ¡Hola!
Mamá: ¿Cómo fue tu primer día en la escuela, Jorge?	Mamá: ¿Cómo fue tu primer día en la escuela, Jorge?
Jorge: Bastante bien.	Jorge: Bastante bien.
Papá: ¿Entiendes todo lo que dicen? ¿Usas tu inglés mucho?	Papá: ¿Entiendes todo lo que dicen? ¿Usas tu inglés mucho?
Jorge: Entiendo la mayoría de lo que dicen. Pero los profesores dicen algunas cosas extrañas.	Jorge: Entiendo la mayoría de lo que dicen. Pero los profesores dicen algunas cosas extrañas.
Mamá: ¿Cómo qué?	Mamá: ¿Cómo qué?
Jorge: Por ejemplo la profesora de ciencias nos dio la tarea y dijo que era un trozo de pastel. No entendí que tenía que ver pastel con la tarea. También el profesor de matemáticas dijo que debemos pegar los libros mucho esta noche. ¡Qué extraño!	Jorge: Por ejemplo la profesora de ciencias nos dio la tarea y dijo que era un trozo de pastel. No entendí que tenía que ver pastel con la tarea. También el profesor de matemáticas dijo que debemos pegar los libros mucho esta noche. ¡Qué extraño!

Solution:

The misunderstanding stems from the teacher's use of American idioms. The science teacher used the phrase "piece of cake" to mean that something is easy and the math teacher asks students to "hit the books" as a way to ask students to study the text. However, idioms are very difficult for language learners. Jorge hears the idioms and interprets them literally. When students encounter English language learners in their community, encourage your students to think of what might be confusing to them and offer assistance.

Standards Targeted: 1.1, 1.2, 1.3, and 4.1

72. ¿Qué pasó? III (Problems with False Cognates)

<table>
<tr><td>

Versión 1:

Estas empresas Americanas no encontraron a buenos traductores para traducir sus anuncios al español. Lee los siguientes anuncios y describe por qué los clientes en Colombia no están interesados en estos productos.

Super Clean Soap:

Para oler bien y estar muy limpio, use la nueva sopa "Super Clean." Esta sopa nueva tiene una fragancia agradable de flores.

Carpets by Pete:

Tenemos gangas buenísimas en carpetas de alta calidad. Usted puede tener carpetas nuevas en toda su casa. ¡Llámenos hoy!

</td><td>

Versión 2:

The following American companies should have hired better translators! Read the following advertisements and see if you can find out why clients in Colombia are not interested in these products.

Super Clean Soap:

Para oler bien y estar muy limpio, use la nueva sopa "Super Clean." Esta sopa nueva tiene una fragancia agradable de flores.

Carpets by Pete:

Tenemos gangas buenísimas en carpetas de alta calidad. Usted puede tener carpetas nuevas en toda su casa. ¡Llámenos hoy!

</td></tr>
</table>

Solution:

These advertisements and companies are made up. However, high-profile translation errors are a reality even in today's business world.

♦ Super Clean Soap: The English word "soap" should be translated as "jabón" and not "sopa" (soup).

♦ Carpets by Pete: The English word "carpet" should be translated as "alfombra" instead of "carpeta" (folder).

Standards Targeted: 1.1, 1.2, and 1.3

73. Ignacio el impaciente

Versión 1:	Versión 2:
Ignacio el impaciente en un estudiante en la clase de español. Desdichadamente, Ignacio trabaja muy rápidamente sin prestar atención a los detalles. Por eso, el trabajo de Ignacio siempre tiene muchos errores. Lee su ensayo y haz las correcciones necesarias.	Ignacio el impaciente is a Spanish student. Unfortunately, he rushes through his work and therefore makes a lot of mistakes. Read the following essay and make corrections.
Hola! Me llamo es Ignacio. Tengo 15 años y mi cumpleños es Marzo 27. Me gusta mucho practicar deportes como baketbal y tenis. Soy muy sociable y me gusta las fiestas y los bailes.	Hola! Me llamo es Ignacio. Tengo 15 años y mi cumpleños es Marzo 27. Me gusta mucho practicar deportes como baketbal y tenis. Soy muy sociable y me gusta las fiestas y los bailes.

Presentation Suggestion:

Because of the alliteration, "Ignacio" works well as the name for the fictitious student in this exercise. However, if you actually have a student named "Ignacio" in your class, use a different name. In the directions, you may also want to let students know that "Ignacio" is a fictitious student.

You can use this type of exercise to review common errors after a test, homework assignment, essay, or other assignment. Create samples for "Ignacio" using errors that your students frequently make. Avoid using samples that are taken word-for-word from a student's work as that can make the student feel embarrassed of their work. Instead, you can use short segments from different students and change elements of the work.

Solution:

¡Hola! Me llamo ~~es~~ Ignacio. Tengo 15 años y mi cumpleaños es **el 27 de marzo**. Me gusta mucho practicar deportes como **básquetbol (o baloncesto)** y tenis. Soy muy sociable y me gus**tan** las fiestas y los bailes.

Standards Targeted: 1.1, 1.2, and 1.3

74. Usando un diccionario

Cuando no sabes una palabra en español (o inglés) ¿qué debes hacer? Una buena idea es usar un diccionario. Es importante saber usar un diccionario. Usa un diccionario español–inglés para responder a las siguientes preguntas.

1. Busca la palabra "backpack" (en inglés)

    ♦ Write down everything included in the entry.

    ♦ What are the different parts of the entry?

    ♦ What do they mean?

2. Busca la palabra "can" (en inglés)

    ♦ What different Spanish word do you find?

    ♦ Which word would you use if you are talking about a container (like a soda can)?

    ♦ How do you know which word to use?

3. Busca la palabra "estoy" (en español)

    ♦ Copy the dictionary entry.

    ♦ What should you do next?

When you don't know a word in Spanish, what should you do? One of the best things to do is use a dictionary to look it up. It is important to know *how* to use a dictionary. Look at a Spanish–English dictionary and answer the following questions.

1. Look up the English word "backpack."

    ♦ Write down everything included in the entry.

    ♦ What are the different parts of the entry?

    ♦ What do they mean?

2. Look up the English word "can."

    ♦ What different Spanish word do you find?

    ♦ Which word would you use if you are talking about a container (like a soda can)?

    ♦ How do you know which word to use?

3. Look up the Spanish word "estoy."

    ♦ Copy the dictionary entry.

    ♦ What should you do next?

Presentation Suggestion:

If possible, provide Spanish–English dictionaries for students to use for this exercise (or ask students to bring their dictionaries to class). If you do not have enough copies to give one to each student, have students work together with a partner or small group.

You may want to use this exercise after some of the other ones in this section that highlight some of the difficulties people sometimes have when translating between languages.

Solution:

1. Answers will vary depending on the specific dictionaries students use. However, most dictionaries should include a pronunciation guide, the translation, part of speech, and gender (as this is a noun). You may want to also ask students to look up a verb so that they can see what is provided for verbs.

2. Answers might include: poder, saber, lata, bote. The word that students should use for a container would be "lata." There are a few strategies students can use to select the correct word. First, they can look at the part of speech for each word. "Lata" is a noun but "poder" and "saber" are verbs. A container (such as you would use for a carbonated beverage) is also a noun. Second, many dictionaries include sample sentences for how you would use each word. These sample selections are usually in bold or italics. Another great technique students can use is to find the words in Spanish and then look them up in the Spanish–English section. If students look up "poder" they will find "to be able to" and lata would say "tin can."

3. Students often attempt to look up conjugated verbs. Most dictionaries will simply list the infinitive of the verb (estar), whereas others will write "see estar." Students should then go to "estar" for additional information.

Variations and Additional Activities:

Many students benefit from instruction on how to use a dictionary. Students may try to look up words (such as conjugated verbs) and then not be able to find translations. Also, students may struggle to select the correct word when there are more than one possible translations.

As a followup, create another list of words for students to translate using dictionaries. Use words that will enrich your class vocabulary lists or that you are going to study in the near future. Provide students with ample opportunities to become acquainted with dictionaries and how to best use them.

Speed Dictionaries:

For this simple game you will need dictionaries for all the students (if you do not have enough, students can work with partners). Give a word in Spanish or English along with a complete sentence. Then ask students to translate the word as it would be used in the sentence. Because the word must be used in the sentence, students will need to conjugate verbs or make adjectives match the words they modify. The first student who can provide the correct answer earns a point.

Instead of selecting the words for the activity, consider asking the students to think of appropriate words that they would like to learn in Spanish. Distribute index cards and ask students to write a word they would like to learn and a sentence using the word. Then use the cards for your class game.

Standards Targeted: 4.1 (1.1, 1.2, and 1.3 indirectly)

75. Femenino/ Masculino

Versión 1:

Probablemente ya sabes que las palabras en español son femeninas o masculinas. ¿Puedes adivinar si una palabra en inglés será femenina o masculina? Adivina si las siguientes palabras son femeninas o masculinas.

1. Dress
2. Tie
3. Makeup
4. Tools

Ahora mira las respuestas. ¿Tienes las respuestas correctas? ¿Puedes adivinar si una palabra en inglés va a ser femenina o masculina en español?

Versión 2:

As you already know, Spanish nouns are either feminine or masculine. Do you think that you can guess which words are feminine or masculine? Look at the following words and guess whether they will be feminine or masculine in Spanish.

1. Dress
2. Tie
3. Makeup
4. Tools

Now, take a look at the answer sheet. Were you right? Can you guess the gender of words if you only know the English word?

Presentation Suggestion:

Place an answer sheet in a central location where students can check their answers before answering the second part of the problem.

Solution:

1. El vestido (masculine)
2. La corbata (feminine)
3. El maquillaje (masculine)
4. Las herramientas (feminine)

Students often believe they can guess whether a word will be feminine or masculine based on whether they believe the object is used primarily by females or males. As this exercise demonstrates, it is *not* possible. When students encounter words that are already in Spanish, remind students that generally words that end in "a" are feminine and words that end in "o" are masculine.

Standards Targeted: 1.1, 1.2, 1.3, and 4.1

A escribir

76. Frases incompletas I

Versión 1:	**Versión 2:**
Termina las siguientes frases. También para cada número añade una o dos frases para explicar tu respuesta.	Finish the following sentences. Also, for each number add a sentence or two to explain your answer.
1. En la tele siempre veo...	1. En la tele siempre veo...
2. Me gusta comer...	2. Me gusta comer...
3. Me gustaría conocer a...	3. Me gustaría conocer a...
4. Mi deporte favorito es...	4. Mi deporte favorito es...
5. Si tengo $100 voy a...	5. Si tengo $100 voy a...

Presentation Suggestion:

Students are often intimidated by the idea of writing a long essay or journal entry in Spanish. Exercises like these can help students begin to feel more comfortable writing in Spanish. Because the beginning of the sentences are provided, even students who are just starting to learn Spanish can complete the activity. For more advanced students, you can reduce the number of sentences and ask them to provide more than one to two sentences of explanation. Also use more complex tenses when appropriate. Modify the sentences to fit what you are currently studying.

Standards Targeted: 1.1, 1.2, and 1.3

77. Frases incompletas II

Versión 1:	**Versión 2:**
Termina las siguientes frases. También para cada número añade una o dos frases para explicar tu respuesta.	Finish the following sentences. Also, for each number add a sentence or two to explain your answer.
1. Un talento que tengo es...	1. Un talento que tengo es...
2. Yo nunca voy a...	2. Yo nunca voy a...
3. Quiero comprar...	3. Quiero comprar...
4. Para la placa en mi automóvil quiero...	4. Para la placa en mi automóvil quiero...
5. Me gusta escuchar...	5. Me gusta escuchar...

Presentation Suggestion:

See above.

Standards Targeted: 1.1, 1.2, and 1.3

78. Mancha de tinta

Preparation:

Copy the following ink blot or project it on the board.

Versión 1:	**Versión 2:**
Mira la mancha de tinta. ¿Qué ves en la mancha? Describe con muchos detalles.	Look at the following ink blot. What can you see? Describe in as much detail as possible.

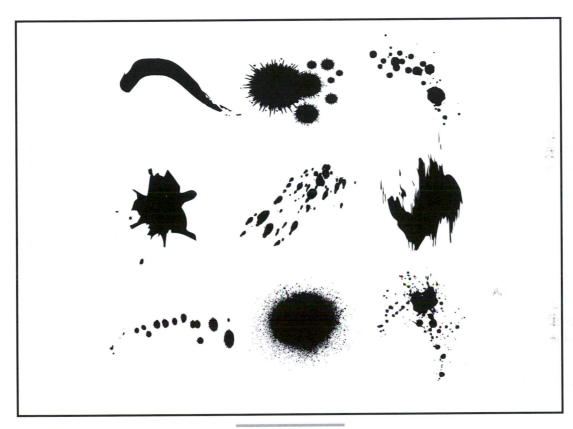

Presentation Suggestion:

The purpose of this activity is to encourage students to generate a lot of language. Depending on your students' level, modify this activity to fit their needs. For beginning students, copy the ink blot and have them label items on the ink blot. Intermediate students could identify items and describe where the items are located. More advanced students could describe what they see and then debate what is in the ink blot with a partner. Regardless of your students' level, encourage them to produce a variety of words and sentences in Spanish. Consider creating your own ink blots that feature the vocabulary you are studying or want to review.

Standards Targeted: 1.1, 1.2, and 1.3

79. Columna de consejos I

Versión 1:	**Versión 2:**
Acabas de empezar un trabajo nuevo escribiendo una columna de consejos en una revista para jóvenes. Escoge una de las siguientes cartas y escribe una respuesta con tus consejos.	You have just been hired to write an advice column for a popular teen magazine. Select one of the letters below and write a short letter with your advice.
Daniela la desordenada:	**Daniela la desordenada:**
Tengo un problema grande—¡soy muy desordenada! Nunca puedo encontrar mis libros en mi armario. Mi dormitorio tiene ropa, papeles y comida por todas partes. ¿Cómo puedo organizarme?	Tengo un problema grande—¡soy muy desordenada! Nunca puedo encontrar mis libros en mi armario. Mi dormitorio tiene ropa, papeles y comida por todas partes. ¿Cómo puedo organizarme?
Timoteo:	**Timoteo:**
Yo quiero ser parte del equipo de fútbol. El año pasado practiqué mucho pero no me aceptaron. No sé si debo intentar otra vez u olvidarme del equipo. Me gusta el fútbol pero no me gusta el rechazo.	Yo quiero ser parte del equipo de fútbol. El año pasado practiqué mucho pero no me aceptaron. No sé si debo intentar otra vez u olvidarme del equipo. Me gusta el fútbol pero no me gusta el rechazo.

Presentation Suggestion:

For beginning students, you may want to provide them with some sentence stems that they can use, such as "Debes..." or "Es importante..." "Pienso que necesitas...."

Variations and Additional Activities:

This activity can easily be modified to fit your curriculum. Modify the letters to include the vocabulary and content you are currently studying. Consider creating a file of advice letters that feature the vocabulary and grammar from each chapter in your curriculum. Then, you can pull those letters and use them as the warmup activity at appropriate times.

As an additional activity, have students write letters describing a problem (real or fictitious). Then have the students exchange their letters with a partner and write responses giving advice to their partners.

Standards Targeted: 1.1, 1.2, and 1.3

80. Columna de consejos II

Versión 1:	Versión 2:
Acabas de empezar un trabajo nuevo escribiendo una columna de consejos en una revista para jóvenes. Escoge una de las siguientes cartas y escribe una respuesta con tus consejos.	You have just been hired to write an advice column for a popular teen magazine. Select one of the letters below and write a short letter with your advice.

Pedro:

Yo comparto mi dormitorio con mi hermanito y es un problema enorme. Mi hermanito siempre está mirando mis cosas, escuchando música tonta, o hablando. ¡Nunca me deja en paz! ¿Qué puedo hacer?

Susana:

Tengo un problema con mi mejor amiga, Clara. Cuando paso tiempo con Clara siempre nos divertimos pero otros amigos dicen que ella habla mal de mí cuando no estoy. ¿Debo hablar sobre esto con Clara? ¿Qué debo hacer?

Pedro:

Yo comparto mi dormitorio con mi hermanito y es un problema enorme. Mi hermanito siempre está mirando mis cosas, escuchando música tonta, o hablando. ¡Nunca me deja en paz! ¿Qué puedo hacer?

Susana:

Tengo un problema con mi mejor amiga, Clara. Cuando paso tiempo con Clara siempre nos divertimos pero otros amigos dicen que ella habla mal de mí cuando no estoy. ¿Debo hablar sobre esto con Clara? ¿Qué debo hacer?

Presentation Suggestion:

For beginning students, you may want to provide them with some sentence stems that they can use, such as "Debes..." or "Es importante..." "Pienso que necesitas...."

Variations and Additional Activities:

This activity can easily be modified to fit your curriculum. Modify the letters to include the vocabulary and content you are currently studying. Consider creating a file of advice letters that feature the vocabulary and grammar from each chapter in your curriculum. Then, you can pull those letters and use them as the warmup activity at appropriate times.

As an additional activity, have students write letters describing a problem (real or fictitious). Then, have the students exchange their letters with a partner and write responses giving advice to their partners.

Standards Targeted: 1.1, 1.2, and 1.3

81. 10 Palabras

Versión 1:	Versión 2:
Hoy vas a escribir un cuento corto. Tu cuento tiene que incluir todas las 10 siguientes palabras. ¡Sé creativo!	Today you are going to write a short story. In your story you must include the following 10 words. Be creative!
1. escuela	1. escuela
2. papas fritas	2. papas fritas
3. cantar	3. cantar
4. Cristóbal Colón	4. Cristóbal Colón
5. interesante	5. interesante
6. vestido	6. vestido
7. amarillo	7. amarillo
8. nadar	8. nadar
9. tarea	9. tarea
10. bicicleta	10. bicicleta

Presentation Suggestion:

Some students might enjoy working alone whereas others might benefit from sharing ideas with a partner. Consider allowing students to work together. After a few minutes, ask students to share their stories. If time permits, you can vote on which story was the most creative, funniest, or most realistic.

Variations and Additional Activities:

This can be a fun way to have students incorporate their new vocabulary words with words they already learned. Change the ten words to fit what you are studying, what students need to review, and other topics of high interest (instead of "Cristóbal Colón" you might want to include a famous person or someone from your school.)

Consider giving students only five words if they are having trouble completing this activity in a reasonable amount of time.

Secret Words:

Do not give students the list of ten words. Instead, ask students to write a short story. Then provide students with a list of the secret words. When you create the list of ten secret words, be creative! Ask students to read through their stories and replace words in their stories with words from your list. Students should note what part of speech each secret word is and use it to replace a word in their story that is the same part of speech. Then ask students to share their stories with the class. Students may enjoy the strange and funny stories that emerge.

Instead of creating the list of ten secret words, have students work with partners. Each student will select ten secret words to give to a partner. After students write their stories, they use their partners' words to replace words in their stories.

Standards Targeted: 1.1, 1.2, and 1.3

82. Director de la escuela

Versión 1:	Versión 2:
Hoy el(la) director(a) de nuestra escuela está enfermo(a). No podemos encontrar a nadie para hacer el trabajo. ¿Podrías tú ser el(la) director(a) hoy? El(la) director(a) de la escuela puede hacer tres reglas nuevas. ¿Qué reglas nuevas harías como director? ¿Por qué?	Hoy el(la) director(a) de nuestra escuela está enfermo(a). No podemos encontrar a nadie para hacer el trabajo. ¿Puedes tú ser el(la) director(a) hoy? Como director(a) de la escuela puedes hacer tres reglas nuevas. ¿Qué reglas nuevas vas a hacer? ¿Por qué?

Presentation Suggestion:

For students who need more assistance, consider providing them with a sample format for their responses (e.g., "Mis reglas nuevas son..." or "Hoy los estudiantes (no) tienen que..."). Encourage students to write in as much detail as possible.

Standards Targeted: 1.1, 1.2, and 1.3

83. Tu vacación ideal

Versión 1:	Versión 2:
Imagínate que puedes tomar una vacación a cualquier lugar que quieras. Puedes hacer lo que te guste. ¿Adónde irías? ¿Qué harías? ¿Con quién viajarías? ¿Por qué? Describe toda tu vacación ideal.	Hoy vas a salir para una vacación ideal. Tienes todo el dinero que necesitas. ¿Adónde vas? ¿Qué vas a hacer? ¿Con quién vas? Describe con muchas detalles.

Presentation Suggestion and Variations:

Although this activity naturally fits with the subjunctive tense, students can also imagine that they are actually going on vacation today and use the present tense; encourage them to use "ir + a + infinitive" or verbs like "pensar" or "querer." For students who need more assistance, consider providing them with a sample format for their responses (e.g., "Para mi vacación voy a..." or "Pienso..."). You could also provide them with a sample paragraph if they need further modeling. Encourage students to write in as much detail as possible.

Standards Targeted: 1.1, 1.2, and 1.3

84. Mi cita

Versión 1:	Versión 2:
Cuando están hablando, muchas personas usan citas de diferentes personas famosas. Por ejemplo, tal vez has oído:	You have probably heard people quote a number of different famous people. For example, you may have heard:

Versión 1:	Versión 2:
"Lo importante es nunca dejar de hacer preguntas." —Albert Einstein	"The important thing is never to stop questioning." —Albert Einstein
"Si lo puedes soñar, lo puedes hacer realidad." —Walt Disney	"If you can dream it,you can make it so." —Walt Disney
"Siempre perderás 100% de las oportunidades que no tomes." —Wayne Gretzky	"You miss 100% of the shots you don't take." —Wayne Gretzky
"La paz empieza con una sonrisa." —La Madre Teresa	"Peace begins with a smile." —Mother Teresa
¡Ahora es tu turno! Escribe una cita original. Imagina que vas a ser conocido(a) por esta cita famosa.	Now it is your turn! Write an original quote that you would like to be known for.

Presentation Suggestion:

Students may have trouble getting started with this exercise as the topic is so broad. If students need a little direction, encourage them to first think of a topic that they know something about, such as a sport, school, friendship, or family. Then ask them to write down a few things that they know about that topic. Using that list they should be able to come up with a quote that illustrates some belief they hold or idea they have.

After students have thought of their quotes, ask them to write their quotes nicely on a full-size sheet of paper or poster. Display the quotes in your room, on a bulletin board, or in the hallway. If time permits, you can have the students take home their papers or posters and add images and designs to their posters. They should model their posters after inspirational posters that they may have seen at school. These quotes may be even more inspiring for your students since they were generated by your students' peers and friends.

Standards Targeted: 1.1, 1.2, and 1.3

85. Un cuento colectivo

Versión 1:	Versión 2:
Hoy vas a escribir un cuento con tus compañeros. Sigue los pasos cuidadosamente. Después de cada paso, dobla tu papel para cubrir lo que escribiste y pasa tu papel a un compañero.	Today you are going to write a story with your classmates! All of your writing must be in Spanish. Follow the steps closely. After each step, fold your paper over to cover your writing and then pass it to a classmate.

Versión 1:

1. Escribe el nombre de tres personas.

2. Escribe "van a" y escribe un lugar y una descripción del lugar.

3. Escribe "Ellos" y describe una acción (usando la forma "ellos" del verbo).

4. Describe un problema. Empieza tu frase con "Ellos tienen…"

5. Escribe, "Entonces, ellos compran…" y termina la frase.

6. Escribe "Al final del día, ellos están" y termina la frase.

Versión 2:

1. Write the names of three people.

2. Write "van a" and a place.

3. Write "Ellos" and then two verbs (make sure to conjugate the verbs in the "ellos" form).

4. Write "Después ellos van a" and another place.

5. Write "Ellos compran" and two things.

6. Write "Allí ellos ven" and a person, thing, or movie title.

7. Write "Al final del día, ellos están" and an adjective (in the plural form).

Presentation Suggestion:

You might want to require students to pass their papers in one direction (resulting in a large circle). If not, students will often hurry to pass their papers to their closest friends. Many students enjoy the funny stories that result from this activity. Depending on your class, you may need to remind students that they can only write school-appropriate stories and sentences. Also, you may want to collect all the stories and read selected ones for the class. Then, you can omit stories that are not enjoyable for all students or that include multiple errors.

Variations and Additional Activities:

There are lots of ways to alter this activity. You can use fewer rules and let the students' creativity really shine! Or, you can use very specific steps and simply change a few items. Also, you can modify the directions so that the chapter vocabulary and the grammatical topics that you are studying is featured.

Standards Targeted: 1.1, 1.2, and 1.3

86. Mis consejos sobre exámenes

Versión 1:	Versión 2:
Te han contratado para hacer un cartel educativo describiendo 10 estrategias para usar cuando tomas exámenes de español. Escribe una lista de consejos que puedes compartir con los demás.	You have been hired to create an educational poster with 10 strategies for taking Spanish tests. Make a list of the best advice that you can share with others.

Presentation Suggestion:

If time permits, have students actually create their posters and hang them in your classroom so that students will have helpful advice during upcoming tests. You may want to do this exercise at the beginning of the year or before an important exam. When returning tests, ask students to review their answers and see if they could have found or corrected some of their errors by using these strategies.

Standards Targeted: 1.1, 1.2, and 1.3

87. Mi resumen del año

Versión 1:	Versión 2:
Escribe cinco frases usando superlativos para describir el año pasado.	Write five sentences using superlatives to describe this past year.
Ejemplo:	**Ejemplo:**
La mejor película del año fue…	La mejor película del año es…

Presentation Suggestion:

This exercise fits well in January (to review the previous calendar year) or at the end of the school year. Instead of reviewing the year, students may want to create a list of superlatives that could be used in a yearbook (such as "best dressed" or "friendliest"). If students create yearbook superlatives, remind students to only write superlatives that are positive in nature.

These statements can be written in the present tense or past tense depending on students' knowledge.

Standards Targeted: 1.1, 1.2, and 1.3

Español en la vida diaria

88. Geografía norteamericana I

Versión 1:	Versión 2:
En los Estados Unidos hay muchos lugares que tienen nombres en Español. ¿Qué significan los siguientes nombres? ¿Sabes dónde se encuentran estos lugares? ¿Son ríos, ciudades, estados, o montañas?	In the United States, many places have Spanish names. Do you know what the following names mean? Do you know where these places are? Are they rivers, cities, states or mountains?

1. Colorado	6. Florida	1. Colorado	6. Florida
2. Los Ángeles	7. Santa Fé	2. Los Ángeles	7. Santa Fé
3. Río Grande	8. Nevada	3. Río Grande	8. Nevada
4. Sangre de Cristo	9. Amarillo	4. Sangre de Cristo	9. Amarillo
5. Las Vegas	10. Montana	5. Las Vegas	10. Montana

Presentation Suggestion:

A large map of the United States, if available, would be a good resource to use with this problem. Students can find the places on the map or show where they think they are. This is a good activity to help students strengthen their geography skills. This part of the problem could also be given as homework or extra credit.

Solution:

1. Colorado: State named after the red-colored clay.

2. Los Ángeles: City in California named for "the angels."

3. Río Grande: literally means "big river."

4. Sangre de Cristo: mountain range in Colorado and New Mexico. The name means "blood of Christ" and was probably named for the red glow on the mountains during sunset.

5. Las Vegas: City in Nevada named for the meadows there.

6. Florida: State named because it was flowered (possibly because of Easter season).

7. Santa Fé: City in New Mexico. Name means "Holy Faith."

8. Nevada: State named after the snow-capped mountains.

9. Amarillo: City in Texas named after yellow soil or yellow wildflowers.

10. Montana: State named after its mountains.

Standards Targeted: 1.1, 1.2, 1.3, 3.1, and 3.2

89. Geografía norteamericana II

Versión 1:	Versión 2:
¿Puedes pensar en algún lugar en los Estados Unidos que tiene un nombre en Español? ¿Qué significa ese nombre?	Can you think of any place in the United States that has a Spanish name? What does that name mean?

Presentation Suggestion:

This exercise would be a good continuation of #88 and you may want to present them in sequence. If students are struggling to think of places with Spanish names, allowing them to look at a map may help. This will also help student further familiarize themselves with U.S. geography.

Solution:

Answers will vary. If students think they have found a place that is named in Spanish but can't figure out the meaning, encourage them to do some investigating and report back to class the following day. If possible, allow students to use dictionaries as they work on this exercise.

Standards Targeted: 1.1, 1.2, 1.3, 3.1, and 3.2

90. Hispanohablantes en Norteamérica

Versión 1:	Versión 2:
En los Estados Unidos, hay muchos hispanohablantes importantes. Piensa en uno(a) y describe por qué esa persona es importante.	There are many important Spanish-speaking people in the United States. Think of one person and describe why they are important.

Presentation Suggestion:

Consider providing a couple of examples to help students get started with this activity.

Variations and Additional Activities:

If time permits, have one student describe the Spanish-speaking person they chose and then have the other students try to guess who it is. The student should describe the person saying, "Estoy pensando en alguien que…" For students with more limited Spanish knowledge they may need to use more simple sentences such as "es cantante." Students can form teams and then take turns presenting to each other. The team that guesses the most wins.

Standards Targeted: 1.1, 1.2, 1.3, and 3.1

91. Música

Versión 1:	Versión 2:
La música latina es muy popular en los Estados Unidos y en todo el mundo. En el año 2000, el canal de CBS estrenó los premios Grammy Latinos. Este programa fue el primer programa de lengua española y portuguesa para estrenar en un canal Americano durante el horario caliente.	Latin music has become extremely popular in the United States and around the world. In 2000, CBS first started airing the Latin Grammy awards. This telecast was groundbreaking as it was the first prime-time show aired on an English network that featured mainly Spanish and Portuguese.
¿Escuchas música latina? ¿A quién te gusta escuchar? ¿Por qué te gusta su música?	Are there any Latin artists that you listen to? What do you like about their music?
Si no te gusta la música latina, ¿conoces algunos artistas latinos?	If you don't like Latin music, who are some artists that you have heard of?
¿En tu opinión, quién ganará premios en los Grammys Latinos este año?	What artists do you think will earn awards at this year's Latin Grammys?

Presentation Suggestion:

If you have the time and resources, play some Latin music for students as they work on this exercise. You could play some of the songs that are nominated for Grammys or show students an excerpt from the awards show.

Additional Information:

The Latin Grammy awards usually air in the beginning of November. You could plan this warmup to coordinate with the Grammys.

Standards Targeted: 1.1, 1.2, 1.3, 3.1, 3.2, 4.2, and 5.1

92. Productos internacionales

Versión 1:	Versión 2:
Sin darte cuenta encuentras productos de todo el mundo cada día. Por ejemplo, si comiste un plátano esta mañana para el desayuno posiblemente comiste un plátano que vino de Costa Rica.	Although you may not realize it, every day you come in contact with products from all around the world. For example, if you ate a banana for breakfast it might have come from Costa Rica.
Mira los objetos que están a tu alrededor. ¿De dónde vienen? Durante las próximas 24 horas haz una lista de los productos que usas y de dónde vienen.	Look through items that you can find nearby. Do they state where they are from? For the next 24 hours, make a note of where the products you use come from.

Presentation Suggestion:

The following day have students create a class list of products they used and where they came from. If you have access to a pin map, you could have students mark what products they used and where they come from.

Additional Information:

A law went into effect on March 16, 2009, that requires many retailers to provide information on where products are from. This is known as "Country of Origin Labeling." Therefore, students should be able to learn where their produce and meat are from. Not all foods (including those that are processed) are included in this law. However, most foods that are sold in their original form are included. If time permits, ask students to think about why consumers feel it is important to know where their foods are from. Encourage students to research this law and some of the issues related to the international sale of foods and products.

Standards Targeted: 1.1, 1.2, 1.3, 2.2, 3.1, and 3.2

Juegos

93. Barajando el vocabulario

Preparation

You will need copies of the game rules and sets of vocabulary pictures. The vocabulary picture sets should include five to ten pictures from the chapter vocabulary. Each picture should be on its own sheet of paper and represent one vocabulary word. The papers can be index cards, half sheets of paper, or full sheets. Make sure that you can't see the pictures through the paper (if you flip over the paper, you shouldn't be able to see the drawing).

Presentation Suggestion:

Students can play this game with partners or small groups.

Students may need to see this game modeled once or twice in order to fully understand the directions. Also, you may want to copy the rules sheet (see following page) so that students can refer to it as they play instead of looking up to read the rules off an overhead projector or the board. Consider reviewing the directions the day before so that as students come into class they can start playing immediately.

You can have pictures of the vocabulary already prepared or can have students create the pictures as a homework assignment the night before. The vocabulary pictures can be on full-size sheets of paper or on smaller papers (index cards tend to work well). If students create the pictures using pen or marker, they may be able to see through the papers. In that case, you will need to provide cardstock or other paper as backing. If not, students will see through the papers and will not be using their memories!

Variations and Additional Activities:

Instead of having students play this game with partners, consider playing the game as a whole class. Place five or six vocabulary cards face up on the board. Ask student what each picture is and make sure they know the words in Spanish. Then, flip over the cards. Slowly move some of the cards to change the order they are in. Ask all of the students to write a list of the five cards in order. Flip over the cards one at a time. Students earn a point for each of the cards they correctly identified. After each round, increase the number of cards you use for the game.

Ask a student to be the "teacher" when playing this game as a whole class. The student can go over the words, flip over the cards, and shuffle some of the cards.

Standards Targeted: 1.1, 1.2, and 1.3

Juego: Barajando el vocabulario

Rules of the game:

1. Select 4 vocabulary pictures and place them on your desk in a line face up.

2. Flip each card over so that the picture side is not visible as shown here.

 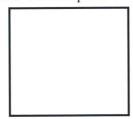  

3. Watch closely as one of you moves some of the cards (you will change what order the cards are in). Try to remember what was on each card and where the cards are now.
   Example:

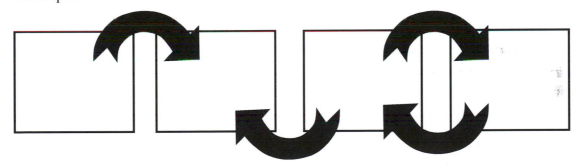

4. The player who did not move the cards begins playing (first player). The first player says what s/he thinks is on a card and then flips it over. For example, s/he says "Creo que es un pez" and flips the card over. If the player was correct and the card has the "pez" (fish) on it, then s/he wins that card. If not, the second player can say what is actually on the card and then the second player wins the card. If the first player answered correctly, s/he continues playing until s/he misses a card.

5. Continue taking turns until all four cards have been turned back over. Once all of the cards are facing up, begin again by turning the cards over and rotating their positions again. You can rotate as many or as few times as you would like!

6. You earn a point for each card that you win. Keep track of your points because at the end of the allotted time, the player with the most points wins!

94. La categoría es...

<table>
<tr><td>

Versión 1:

Hoy vas a jugar un juego breve para empezar la clase. Siéntate con tu pareja o grupo. Necesitas un papel en blanco para la actividad. Vas a recibir una categoría de tu profesor(a), por ejemplo "comidas." Cada jugador va a tomar un turno escribiendo una palabra en español que pertenece a esa categoría (por ejemplo, "uvas" o "mantequilla"). Si alguien no puede pensar en una palabra o escribe una palabra que ya está en la lista, esa persona está eliminada del juego. El juego continua hasta que nadie pueda añadir más palabras. La persona que escribió la última palabra gana. ¡Buena suerte!

</td><td>

Versión 2:

Today you will begin class with a short game. Sit with your group or partner. You need one blank paper for your group. Your teacher will give you a category such as "Comidas." Then each of you will take a turn writing a Spanish word on your paper that fits the category (e.g., "uvas" or "mantequilla"). If a player cannot think of a word or adds a word that is already on the list, that player is eliminated. Play continues until no one can add any more words. The person who added the last word to the list wins. Good luck!

</td></tr>
</table>

Presentation Suggestion:

To help students understand the directions, you may want to quickly model a round of this game. If you are under tight time constraints, model the activity for the last one or two minutes of class one day and have the students complete the activity the following day as their warmup activity.

You can assign all the groups the same category or use different categories. Also, consider asking students to think of their own categories. With advanced students, you want to make sure the category is not too broad or the game can take too long. Some sample categories:

- ◆ animals at the zoo
- ◆ things in a normal locker
- ◆ five-syllable words
- ◆ irregular verbs
- ◆ things that are green

You may want to add the rule that if a player spells a word incorrectly, the player is eliminated. That forces students to think carefully about how to spell their vocabulary words.

Variations and Additional Activities:

This game can be a lot of fun for the whole class to play together. Divide the class into teams. Each team should have a section of the chalkboard/whiteboard. The teams take turns writing words. Again, no team can write a word that is already on the board. The students will learn quickly that they need to whisper in their groups so that other teams don't steal their words.

Standards Targeted: 1.1, 1.2, and 1.3

95. Veo, Veo

Versión 1:	Versión 2:
En inglés mucha gente juega "I spy" pero en español la gente juega "Veo, veo." Vas a jugar con una pareja. Estudiante 1 empieza y escoge un objeto en la clase (pero es un secreto). Estudiante 2 tiene que adivinar qué es. Deben leer las siguientes oraciones juntos:	You might have played "I spy" before. In Spanish, people play "Veo, Veo." Select a partner to play with. Then, Student 1 begins by selecting an object in the classroom (but don't tell your partner!). Student 2 must guess what the object is. Go through the following rhyme together.

Versión 1 (cont.)	Versión 2 (cont.)
1. Veo veo.	1. Veo veo.
2. ¿Qué ves?	2. ¿Qué ves?
1. Una cosa maravillosa.	1. Una cosa maravillosa.
2. ¿De qué color?	2. ¿De qué color?
1. De color...	1. De color...

| Ahora, estudiante 2 tiene que continuar haciendo preguntas con respuestas de sí/no hasta que pueda adivinar la cosa secreta. Toma nota de cuantas preguntas necesita para adivinar la cosa secreta. Después, estudiante 2 piensa en una cosa y estudiante 1 adivina. | Now, Student 2 should continue by asking yes/no questions until s/he can guess what the object is. Keep track of how many questions Student 2 needed to guess the object. Then, trade roles. |

Presentation Suggestion:

This game works well between partners, small groups, or the whole class. For variety, consider playing with different configurations.

Additional Information:

In some Spanish-speaking countries, the way this game is played is slightly different. For example, some people don't give the color but instead say "empieza con la letra...."

Standards Targeted: 1.1, 1.2, 1.3, and 2.1

96. Bingo

Preparation:
Copy the bingo boards. You may also want to have students create clue cards in advance (see below).

Versión 1:	Versión 2:
Hoy vas a jugar bingo. Escribe tu vocabulario en la tarjeta de Bingo. Escribe una palabra en cada espacio Una persona va a leer pistas. Tacha el espacio con la palabra que encaja con la pista. Cuando tienes 5 palabras tachadas en una línea (horizontal, vertical, o diagonal) grita "¡Bingo!" ¡Buena suerte!	Today you are going to play bingo. Begin by writing your vocabulary words onto the bingo board. Place one word in each space. The bingo caller will read a clue. Cross off the space with the vocabulary word that matches the clue. When you have 5 words in a row (horizontal, vertical, or diagonal) shout out "Bingo!" ¡Buena suerte!

Presentation Suggestion:

Initially, it may seem that bingo would take too long to use as a warmup problem. However, with some simple modifications it can be an ideal way to start class (and take less than five minutes!). If you have students who tend to come to class right as the bell rings or even a little bit late, a game can really motivate them to make it to class on time.

You can give students the bingo boards at the beginning of class or the day before. The students should fill in the bingo boards with their chapter vocabulary (one word per space). If it takes your students a long time to fill in the words, you will want to assign that as part of the homework the night before.

Create clue cards or have the students write clue cards as a homework assignment. The clue cards should have descriptions, in Spanish, for the vocabulary words, such as "Es una fruta roja. Crece en los árboles." Depending on your students' level, you may want to use pictures or some other clue. Instead of reading the clue cards yourself, you can ask a student to be the bingo caller. Then, you are free to complete your attendance, talk to students, or take care of other important tasks while the students complete the activity.

Variations and Additional Activities:

Instead of playing as a whole class, students can play in small groups. The students can place the clue cards in a pile on their desks. Then, they take turns flipping over the clue cards and reading them. With this variation you will either need to prepare clue card sets in advance or assign this to your students.

Standards Targeted: 1.1, 1.2, and 1.3

Bingo Board

		¡Gratis!		

97. La Piñata

Rules of the game:

♦ This game is played between two people, the drawer and the guesser.

♦ The drawer selects a vocabulary word (example: escuela) and draws spaces for each letter:

- - - - - - -

♦ The guesser must guess what letters are in the word. The player would say, "¿Hay una...?" (example, "¿Hay una s?")

♦ If the guesser was correct, the drawer must fill that letter in on the spaces.

- s - - - - -

♦ If the guess was incorrect the drawer draws one piece of the piñata (see below).

♦ Play continues with the guesser suggesting additional letters. If the guesser can figure out the word before the drawer completes the piñata, the guesser wins. If the drawer finishes the piñata before the guesser knows the word, the drawer wins.

Drawing a piñata:

Basically, you just need to be able to draw a circle and six triangles. Draw the circle first and then add a triangle for each additional mistake.

Presentation Suggestion:

This game is almost identical to a game some students may have previously played ("hangman"). You may want to copy the rules for your students or go over them with your students. In addition to single words, students can use phrases for their puzzles. Consider requiring students to use the chapter vocabulary. As an added challenge, implement the rule that once a student guesses the word she must be able to define it in Spanish to win.

Standards Targeted: 1.1, 1.2, and 1.3

98. Memoria

Preparation:

You will need 20 index cards per group.

Versión 1:

Hoy vas a jugar memoria con una pareja. Primero, necesitas 20 tarjetas. En 10 de las tarjetas vas a escribir una palabra de tu vocabulario. En las otras 10 tarjetas necesitas escribir una definición (¡en español!) de las palabras que escribiste.

Cuando terminas haciendo las tarjetas, voltéalas y ponlas en la mesa. Van a tomar turnos volteando 2 tarjetas. Si las tarjetas encajan (tienes la palabra de vocabulario y la definición), te quedas con las tarjetas y tomas otro turno. Al final del juego el jugador con la mayoría de las tarjetas gana.

Versión 2:

You are going to play a game of memory today with your partner. First, you need 20 index cards. On 10 of the index cards you are going to write vocabulary words. On the other 10 you are going to draw pictures for the vocabulary words.

Once you have finished creating your cards, turn them all face down on your table. Take turns flipping over two cards. If the cards match (you turn over the vocabulary word and matching picture), you keep the cards and take another turn. At the end of the game, the player with the most matches wins.

Presentation Suggestion:

Instead of having students create their memory cards in class, you could have them make the cards as homework. Then, students could begin playing immediately when they arrive. You could also create the memory sets and give them to students.

Variation:

Instead of having students match the vocabulary word with a picture or the definition you could have students match:

- ◆ vocabulary word *with* synonyms

- ◆ vocabulary word *with* antonyms

- ◆ vocabulary word *with* a sentence that has the word omitted

- ◆ vocabulary word *with* a picture word

Standards Targeted: 1.1, 1.2, and 1.3

99. Tic-Tac-Toe

Versión 1:

Vas a jugar tic-tac-toe hoy. Pero, para tomar tu turno tienes que escribir la forma correcta del verbo en el espacio. Si hay un error en tu verbo pierdes tu turno. La primera persona que tiene tres en una fila ¡gana!

Versión 2:

Today you are going to play tic-tac-toe. However, to take your turn, you have to write the correct verb form in the space. If there is an error in your verb, you lose a turn. The first person to have three in a row wins!

Usted	Yo	Ustedes
Ellos	Ella	Tú
Él	Ellas	Nosotros

Ellos	Tú	Ustedes
Nosotros	Yo	Ella
Él	Ellas	Usted

Presentation Suggestion:

Before beginning, make sure that all the students know how to play tic-tac-toe. The rules of the game are simple. Players take turns marking a space with either an "X" or an "O." The goal is to be the first person with three spaces in a row. With this variation, students must write the correct Spanish verb in the space (conjugated based on the subject pronoun that is written in that space); if they write the verb incorrectly they lose their turn. If all nine spaces are filled but no one has three in a row it is a tie game.

You may want to provide students with a list of verbs that they should use for this game. Also, require students to use the tense that you are currently studying.

If you have a classroom set of white boards this is a great time to use them so that students can play multiple rounds quickly. You can set up the boards with a wet-erase marker and then the students use dry-erase markers to play. After each round the students can erase their answers but still have the tic-tac-toe board to use. Also, you can copy the tic-tac-toe boards and then laminate them. With most lamination students can write on the lamination using dry-erase markers or crayons and then erase their marks.

Standards Targeted: 1.1, 1.2, and 1.3

100. ¿Dónde están las vocales?

Versión 1:	Versión 2:
Todas las vocales desaparecieron de las siguientes palabras. Añade vocales a las consonantes para crear diferentes palabras. No puedes añadir consonantes o cambiar el orden de las consonantes—sólo puedes añadir vocales.	Somehow all of the vowels have disappeared from the following words. Add vowels to the following consonants to see how many different words you can make. You cannot change the order of the consonants—you can only add vowels.

Ejemplo: sl

Palabras: sal, sala, solo, sólo, sol

1. lg
2. mr
3. q
4. rt
5. ps

Ejemplo: sl

Words: sal, sala, solo, sólo, sol

1. lg
2. mr
3. q
4. rt
5. ps

Variations and Additional Activities:

If your students thrive on competition, you can have individuals or groups compete to see who can come up with the most words. Then students can also write consonant combinations and challenge other teams to find words by adding vowels. You may want to limit students to between one and three consonants (with more than three, there are typically only one or two possible answers).

Modify this activity to include words from your vocabulary. This activity can be used repeatedly if you modify the consonants that you give students.

Solution:

Some possible answers include the following:
1. algo, lago, luego
2. mar, amor, amar
3. qué, que, aquí
4. rata, arte, rato, roto, reto
5. pasa, pasó, país, puso

Standards Targeted: 1.1, 1.2, and 1.3

101. Buscapalabras – Comida

Preparation:

Copy student word search.

Presentation Suggestion:

After a few minutes, have students compare their lists. If you would like, you declare the student with the most words the "winner." Also, after students find the words you can have them create pictures of the words or write sentences with the words. Instead of using this word search (or #102) create puzzles that feature your chapter vocabulary. Consider developing a file of word searches for each chapter that you teach.

Solution:

```
T  P  O  L  L  O  H  V  M  A  N  Z  A  N  A  C  Z  A  P  N
H  E  L  A  D  O  V  N  T  M  B  E  R  O  R  Ú  B  G  T  P
S  R  J  V  Q  O  C  U  M  K  O  S  Ó  L  Á  L  K  U  N  O
M  A  C  S  P  F  R  E  S  A  S  M  E  R  N  E  B  A  S  Q
Ó  L  C  U  G  Z  E  T  H  L  E  T  E  M  D  C  P  J  L  M
M  Y  N  G  U  V  A  E  S  P  T  N  A  R  A  N  J  A  P  A
Y  N  T  S  I  I  Y  O  N  C  O  J  M  F  N  H  T  Y  I  N
S  B  G  P  S  J  B  I  S  T  E  C  K  F  O  J  F  U  Z  T
A  Z  N  B  A  X  A  S  E  L  A  L  V  L  G  P  J  G  Z  E
N  I  Á  M  N  N  U  L  E  C  H  U  G  A  J  Y  A  P  N  Q
D  Q  T  C  T  N  P  Z  S  R  B  P  Y  N  M  L  M  A  X  U
Í  N  E  L  E  C  H  E  C  R  Z  T  T  M  E  L  Ó  N  M  I
A  Q  T  R  S  V  T  A  P  L  E  Í  L  E  P  E  N  R  O  L
D  M  A  R  I  S  C  O  S  Q  S  H  I  L  V  É  R  M  Z  L
Z  S  D  L  S  W  I  P  L  Á  T  A  N  O  C  L  I  H  C  A
O  S  Z  T  O  V  E  I  V  R  P  T  O  M  A  T  E  L  E  D
Í  S  M  O  C  E  J  Ñ  W  S  N  Ú  Y  A  T  S  L  Ú  O  M
E  Q  U  E  S  O  L  A  Q  Z  Y  N  S  Q  W  A  S  O  M  E
R  N  E  E  S  D  H  U  E  V  O  S  B  C  I  S  O  P  A  S
```

Hidden Words:

Agua	Bistec	Guisantes	Jamón	Manzana	Naranja	Piña	Queso
Arándano	Flan	Helado	Leche	Mariscos	Pan	Plátano	Sandía
Atún	Fresas	Huevos	Mantequilla	Melón	Pera	Pollo	Sopa

Standards Targeted: 1.1, 1.2, and 1.3

Buscapalabras – La comida

See how many food words you can find in the following word search. Circle or highlight the words you find and then list them below.

```
T  P  O  L  L  O  H  V  M  A  N  Z  A  N  A  C  Z  A  P  N
H  E  L  A  D  O  V  N  T  M  B  E  R  O  R  Ú  B  G  T  P
S  R  J  V  Q  O  C  U  M  K  O  S  Ó  L  Á  L  K  U  N  O
M  A  C  S  P  F  R  E  S  A  S  M  E  R  N  E  B  A  S  Q
Ó  L  C  U  G  Z  E  T  H  L  E  T  E  M  D  C  P  J  L  M
M  Y  N  G  U  V  A  E  S  P  T  N  A  R  A  N  J  A  P  A
Y  N  T  S  I  I  Y  O  N  C  O  J  M  F  N  H  T  Y  I  N
S  B  G  P  S  J  B  I  S  T  E  C  K  F  O  J  F  U  Z  T
A  Z  N  B  A  X  A  S  E  L  A  L  V  L  G  P  J  G  Z  E
N  I  Á  M  N  N  U  L  E  C  H  U  G  A  J  Y  A  P  N  Q
D  Q  T  C  T  N  P  Z  S  R  B  P  Y  N  M  L  M  A  X  U
I  N  E  L  E  C  H  E  C  R  Z  T  T  M  E  L  Ó  N  M  I
A  Q  T  R  S  V  T  A  P  L  E  Í  L  E  P  E  N  R  O  L
D  M  A  R  I  S  C  O  S  Q  S  H  I  L  V  É  R  M  Z  L
Z  S  D  L  S  W  I  P  L  Á  T  A  N  O  C  L  I  H  C  A
O  S  Z  T  O  V  E  I  V  R  P  T  O  M  A  T  E  L  E  D
Í  S  M  O  C  E  J  Ñ  W  S  N  Ú  Y  A  T  S  L  Ú  O  M
E  Q  U  E  S  O  L  A  Q  Z  Y  N  S  Q  W  A  S  O  M  E
R  N  E  E  S  D  H  U  E  V  O  S  B  C  I  S  O  P  A  S
```

Hidden Words:

102. Buscapalabras – La ropa

Preparation:

Copy student word search.

Presentation Suggestion:

After a few minutes, have students compare their lists. If you would like, you can declare the student with the most words the "winner." Also, after students find the words you can have them create pictures of the words or write sentences with the words. Instead of using this word search (or #101), create puzzles that feature your chapter vocabulary. Consider developing a file of word searches for each chapter that you teach.

Solution:

```
G O R R A U S N X Y M B A C Ó P Z A P N
E L N Ó H G Ú E C D I U N U V A Í G T P
A C Z A P A T O S A X F J P L N N U N O
Z S F P V O J G L Q E A J C O T Q A S Q
C H A Q U E T A N Ú G N T I S A L J L M
A D B S L T A F A R G D E N U L Y A P F
L M E C C Z P A M D B A O T C O L V I A
C I L M O R F S Ó N L F X U J N O T F L
E H U G R E C A B R I G O R I E U M E D
T X A Ú B Í H V L E B U M Ó Y S J A Ó A
I Y M M A T V Q U Q A C N X R Ú L E C
N D B O T A S E S J E N F H I N S L O D
E P Ó J A J E P A M Ú T E U G E R A X Y
S G N U L M H Z J Y H E L I J Y B J T O
Í N Q B E J O Y A S D S E F A Í D I R G
A R C S N D N N Í S Ó E B N P F A Q A L
S U É T E R Ú T S E D C A M I S A L J A
P F Z H S X K G V Y R B R Ó E U G S E Í
L V E S T I D O Z E A L D C T G E Z M H
```

Hidden Words:

Abrigo	Bufanda	Chaqueta	Falda	Guantes	Suéter	Zapatos
Blusa	Calcetines	Cinturón	Gafas	Joyas	Traje	
Botas	Camisa	Corbata	Gorra	Pantalones	Vestido	

Standards Targeted: 1.1, 1.2, and 1.3

Buscapalabras – La ropa

See how many clothing words you can find in the following word search. Circle or highlight the words you find and then list them below.

```
G  O  R  R  A  U  S  N  X  Y  M  B  A  C  Ó  P  Z  A  P  N
E  L  N  Ó  H  G  Ú  E  C  D  I  U  N  U  V  A  Í  G  T  P
A  C  Z  A  P  A  T  O  S  A  X  F  J  P  L  N  N  U  N  O
Z  S  F  P  V  O  J  G  L  Q  E  A  J  C  O  T  Q  A  S  Q
C  H  A  Q  U  E  T  A  N  Ú  G  N  T  I  S  A  L  J  L  M
A  D  B  S  L  T  A  F  A  R  G  D  E  N  U  L  Y  A  P  F
L  M  E  C  C  Z  P  A  M  D  B  A  O  T  C  O  L  V  I  A
C  I  L  M  O  R  F  S  Ó  N  L  F  X  U  J  N  O  T  F  L
E  H  U  G  R  E  C  A  B  R  I  G  O  R  I  E  U  M  E  D
T  X  A  Ú  B  Í  H  V  L  E  B  U  M  Ó  Y  S  J  A  Ó  A
I  Y  M  M  A  T  V  Q  U  U  Q  A  C  N  X  R  Ú  L  E  C
N  D  B  O  T  A  S  E  S  J  E  N  F  H  I  N  S  L  O  D
E  P  Ó  J  A  J  E  P  A  M  Ú  T  E  U  G  E  R  A  X  Y
S  G  N  U  L  M  H  Z  J  Y  H  E  L  I  J  Y  B  J  T  O
Í  N  Q  B  E  J  O  Y  A  S  D  S  E  F  A  Í  D  I  R  G
A  R  C  S  N  D  N  N  Í  S  Ó  E  B  N  P  F  A  Q  A  L
S  U  É  T  E  R  Ú  T  S  E  D  C  A  M  I  S  A  L  J  A
P  F  Z  H  S  X  K  G  V  Y  R  B  R  Ó  E  U  G  S  E  Í
L  V  E  S  T  I  D  O  Z  E  A  L  D  C  T  G  E  Z  M  H
```

Hidden Words:

103. Preguntas, preguntas

Versión 1:	Versión 2:
Vas a jugar este juego con un compañero. Primero, escribe una palabra de tu vocabulario en un papel. ¡Tu palabra es un secreto! Ahora, tu compañero tiene que adivinar tu palabra secreta pero solo puede hacer preguntas de sí/no (la respuesta a las preguntas siempre tiene que ser simplemente sí/no). Toma nota de cuantas preguntas tu compañero hace antes de adivinar tu palabra. Después es tu turno para adivinar la palabra secreta de tu compañero. La persona que necesita menos preguntas para adivinar la palabra gana. ¡Buena suerte!	You are going to play this game with a partner. First, write a word from the vocabulary you are currently studying on a piece of paper. Your word is a secret so don't tell anyone. Now, your partner needs to guess your secret word but s/he can only ask yes/no questions (the answer to the question can only be yes or no). Tally how many questions your partner asks before guessing your word. Then it is your turn to guess your partner's secret word. The person who guesses the correct word with the fewest number of questions wins. Good luck!

Presentation Suggestion:

This game is very similar to "21 questions," which students may have played as children. Some students who haven't played a lot of these types of games may not immediately think of good strategies for this game. Encourage students to begin by looking at the vocabulary and grouping the words into big categories (such as "Is it a verb?" or "Is it a food?"). This will help students narrow down the topics but also will help students think about categorizing and grouping the vocabulary that they are studying! Before beginning, you may want to remind students of how to pose questions correctly in Spanish.

Variations and Additional Activities:

Instead of having the students select the word, write the vocabulary words on index cards. The students then draw a card from the pile. This can sometimes help the game move more quickly if you have students who would take a long time to select their word. Also, this might help if students are particularly creative in selecting their words.

Instead of having students select words from the current chapter, you could allow them to select any word that they have previously studied.

This game works well with partners but can also be played in small groups or as a whole-class activity. Consider playing a round or two with the whole class so the students understand the rules and then have students play with partners.

Standards Targeted: 1.1, 1.2, and 1.3

Conexiones

Activities that help students connect Spanish
with other disciplines (the arts, social sciences,
mathematics, and science are included)

104. Pinturas famosas

Mira la siguiente lista de pinturas famosas. ¿Sabes quién pintó cada pintura? Si necesitas ayuda, mira la lista de pintores y usa la lista para emparejar los pintores con sus pinturas.

Pinturas:

♦ La persistencia de la memoria

♦ Vista de Toledo

♦ Diego y Yo

♦ Guernica

♦ Las Meninas

Pintores:

♦ El Greco

♦ Diego Velásquez

♦ Pablo Picasso

♦ Salvador Dalí

♦ Frida Kahlo

Look at the following list of famous paintings? Do you know who painted each of the paintings? If you need help, look at the list of artists and try to match the artists with their paintings.

Pinturas:

♦ La persistencia de la memoria

♦ Vista de Toledo

♦ Diego y Yo

♦ Guernica

♦ Las Meninas

Pintores:

♦ El Greco

♦ Diego Velásquez

♦ Pablo Picasso

♦ Salvador Dalí

♦ Frida Kahlo

Presentation Suggestion:

If you have copies of these works (or can display them on an overhead or LCD projector) consider showing them to the students as they work on this exercise. As a followup activity, encourage students to find out a few interesting facts about these works or the artists.

Modify the activity to include other works of art or artists. Consider using famous works that are featured in your textbook or curriculum or works that relate to the theme you are studying.

Solution:

La persistencia de la memoria = Salvador Dalí
Vista de Toledo = El Greco
Diego y Yo = Frida Kahlo
Guernica = Pablo Picasso
Las Meninas = Diego Velásquez

Standards Targeted: 1.1, 1.2, 1.3, 3.1, and 3.2

105. Tus gustos

Versión 1:	Versión 2:
El arte puede tomar muchas formas diferentes como escultura, pintura, danza o música. ¿Qué tipo de arte te gusta crear? ¿Qué tipo de arte de gusta ver o escuchar? ¿Por qué?	Art can take a variety of forms, such as sculpture, painting, dance, or music. Do you have a favorite type of art to create? Do you have a favorite type of art to look at or listen to? Why do you like these art forms?

Presentation Suggestion:

Encourage students to think about a wide variety of art forms. You may want to display some images of different types of art to help students think creatively. If your students have experience working with these different art forms, encourage them to share their work (or pictures of their work) with the class.

Standards Targeted: 1.1, 1.2, 1.3, 3.1, and 3.2

106. Mirando una obra de arte

Preparation:

This activity requires students to examine a piece of artwork closely. Select a piece that you find interesting or appropriate based on what you are studying. You may want to select a piece that is copied in your textbook so that your students can look in their own books. Alternately, consider displaying the image on a poster, overhead projector, or LCD projector. Select student questions from the following lists.

Versión 1:	Versión 2:
Mira la obra de arte y responde a las siguientes preguntas.	Look carefully at the selected piece of art and answer the following questions.
1. ¿Qué colores usa el artista? ¿Por qué crees que el artista escogió esos colores?	1. What colors does the artist use? Why do you think the artist selected those colors?
2. Escoge una persona de la pintura y descríbela. Si prefieres, puedes escoger un objeto.	2. Choose a person from the painting and describe him/her. If you prefer, you can select an object.
3. ¿Te gusta esta pintura? ¿Por qué?	3. Do you like this painting? Why or why not?

Presentation Suggestion:

After students have time to respond to the painting, engage the students in a class discussion or group discussions.

Standards Targeted: 1.1, 1.2, 1.3, 3.1, and 3.2

107. Mirando una obra de arte II

Preparation:

This activity requires students to examine a piece of artwork closely. Select a piece that you find interesting or appropriate based on what you are studying. You may want to select a piece that is copied in your textbook so that your students can look in their own books. Alternately, consider displaying the image on a poster, overhead projector, or LCD projector. Select student questions from the following lists.

Versión 1:	Versión 2:
Mira la obra de arte y responde a las siguientes preguntas.	Look carefully at the selected piece of art and answer the following questions.
1. ¿Qué está pasando en esta obra de arte?	1. What is happening in this painting?
2. ¿La obra se parece a la vida real? ¿Por qué crees que el artista pintó su imagen de esta manera?	2. Is this painting realistic? If not, why do you think the artist painted it this way?
3. ¿Te gusta esta pintura? ¿Por qué?	3. Do you like this painting? Why or why not?

Presentation Suggestion:

After students have time to respond to the painting, engage the students in a class discussion or group discussions.

Standards Targeted: 1.1, 1.2, 1.3, 3.1, and 3.2

108. El arte es una mentira...

Versión 1:	Versión 2:
El famoso artista Pablo Picasso dijo, "El arte es una mentira que nos acerca a la verdad." ¿Qué piensas que significa esta cita? ¿Piensas que tiene sentido? ¿Por qué?	Pablo Picasso, a famous artist, once said, "Art is a lie that brings us closer to the truth." What do you think this quote means? Do you think that it makes sense? Why?

Presentation Suggestion:

Depending on your students' levels, consider having students discuss the quote with partners and then engage the students in a whole-class discussion.

Solution:

Answers will vary. Encourage students to think about the meaning of art.

Standards Targeted: 1.1, 1.2, 1.3, and 3.1

109. Un agente de viajes

Versión 1:	Versión 2:
Trabajas como agente de viajes. Uno de tus clientes quiere viajar por Sudamérica y visitar las siguientes ciudades:	You work as a travel agent. One of your clients wants to tour South America and see the following cities:

Versión 1:

Trabajas como agente de viajes. Uno de tus clientes quiere viajar por Sudamérica y visitar las siguientes ciudades:

♦ Caracas, Venezuela

♦ Asunción, Paraguay

♦ Montevideo, Uruguay,

♦ Bogotá, Colombia,

♦ Lima, Perú

♦ Santiago, Chile

Tienes que planear una ruta lógica para tu cliente. ¿En qué orden debe tu cliente visitar cada ciudad?

Versión 2:

You work as a travel agent. One of your clients wants to tour South America and see the following cities:

♦ Caracas, Venezuela

♦ Asunción, Paraguay

♦ Montevideo, Uruguay,

♦ Bogotá, Colombia,

♦ Lima, Perú

♦ Santiago, Chile

You need to plan a logical route for our client. In what order should the client travel to each of those cities?

Presentation Suggestion:

Modify the cities to feature locations that you have studied recently or are going to include in your curriculum.

As a followup question you could ask students: What methods of transportation could your client use to travel between these cities? (¿Cuáles métodos de transporte puede usar tu cliente para viajar entre estas ciudades?)

Variations and Additional Activities:

Have students find partners. One student (the tourist) should select four to five Spanish-speaking cities. Then the tourist should give the list of cities to the travel agent (the other student). The travel agent needs to recommend routes and different methods of transportation to the client. Require students to speak exclusively in Spanish about their travel plans. If necessary, provide students with a list of appropriate travel vocabulary or sentence stems.

Solution:

Answers will vary. Encourage students to use a map to plan logical routes. In going over the answers, you may want to have students use a map to demonstrate their routes.

Standards Targeted: 1.1, 1.2, 1.3, 3.1, and 3.2

110. En orden cronológico

Preparation:

The activity found on the next page can be photocopied, displayed on a projector or copied onto a chalkboard/whiteboard. Select the method that works best for your classroom.

Solution:

1. D (1492)	4. A (1810)	7. G (1898)	10. C (1959)
2. J (1521)	5. H (1846-1848)	8. E (1914)	
3. F (1532)	6. B (1864-1870)	9. I (1929)	

Events Listed in Chronological Order:
(use this list if playing the following game version)

D. Colón llega al nuevo mundo. (1492)

J. Hernán Cortés y los españoles conquistan Tenochtitlan (1521)

F. Francisco Pizarro captura a Atahualpa, el líder del imperio Inca (1532)

A. México declara su independencia de España. (1810)

H. La intervención estadounidense (conocida en Norteamérica como "Mexican American War") (1846–1848)

B. Brasil, Uruguay y Argentina (La Triple Alianza) lucharon contra Paraguay en una guerra (1864)

G. La Guerra Hispano-Americana (conocida en Norteamérica como "The Spanish American War") (1898)

E. La inauguración del Canal de Panamá (1914)

I. Las mujeres reciben el derecho a votar en Ecuador (1929)

C. Fidel Castro llega al poder en Cuba (1959)

Variations and Additional Activities:

Juego: ¿Antes – después - entre? Ask students to form small groups (three to five students). One student is the fair judge and the other students will be playing the game. Each judge will need a copy of the answer sheet. Each group also needs a blank sheet of paper (or a small white board).

The judge begins by drawing a line across the paper and writing the letter "A" in the center of the paper. This is the beginning of the student timeline. The students need to read the statement out loud together.

The first player must decide if statement "B" occurred before or after "A." The player states "Esto ocurrió antes/después…." If the player is correct, he writes it on the timeline and it is the next player's turn. If the player is incorrect he does not write anything on the timeline and it is the following player's turn. Students continue taking

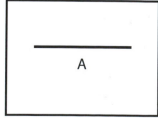

turns and adding events to the timeline. As more events are listed on the timeline, students must specify whether new events occurred before, after, or between other events on the timeline. At the end of the game, the student who wrote the most events on the timeline wins.

Standards Targeted: 1.1, 1.2, 1.3, 3.1, and 3.2

En orden cronológico (versión 1)

Pon los siguientes 10 eventos en orden cronológico.

A. México declara su independencia de España

B. Brasil, Uruguay y Argentina (La Triple Alianza) lucharon contra Paraguay en una guerra

C. Fidel Castro llega al poder en Cuba

D. Colón llega al nuevo mundo

E. La inauguración del Canal de Panamá

F. Francisco Pizarro captura a Atahualpa, el líder del imperio Inca

G. La Guerra Hispano-Americana (conocida en Norteamérica como "The Spanish American War")

H. La intervención estadounidense (conocida en Norteamérica como "Mexican American War")

I. Las mujeres reciben el derecho a votar en Ecuador

J. Hernán Cortés y los españoles conquistan Tenochtitlan

En orden cronológico (versión 2)

Put the following 10 events in chronological order.

A. Mexico declares its independence from Spain

B. Brazil, Uruguay, and Argentina (The Triple Alliance) fight against Paraguay in a war

C. Fidel Castro becomes the leader of Cuba

D. Columbus reaches the New World

E. The inauguration of the Panama Canal

F. Francisco Pizarro captures the leader of the Incan empire, Atahualpa

G. The Spanish–American War

H. The Mexican–American War

I. Woman are given the right to vote in Ecuador

J. Hernán Cortés and the Spaniards conquer Tenochtitlan

111. Los aztecas, incas y mayas

Versión 1:	Versión 2:
Lee las siguientes oraciones sobre los aztecas, incas y mayas. ¿Son verdaderas o falsas?	Read the following statements about the Aztecs, Incas, and Mayas. Mark whether each statement is true or false.

Versión 1:

1. Los aztecas construyeron muchas cosas famosas como chinampas y pirámides.

2. Los aztecas tenían presidentes y el más famoso se llamaba Francisco Vásquez de Coronado.

3. Los mayas jugaban un juego con una pelota y tenían que pasar la pelota por un círculo. Las mujeres y los niños jugaban mucho.

4. Los incas vivían al oeste de Sudamérica. Dos de sus ciudades famosas son Cuzco y Machu Pichu.

5. Hernán Cortés conquistó los aztecas y Francisco Pizarro conquistó los incas.

Versión 2:

1. Los aztecas construyeron muchas cosas famosas como chinampas y pirámides.

2. Los aztecas tenían presidentes y el más famoso se llamaba Francisco Vásquez de Coronado.

3. Los mayas jugaban un juego con una pelota y tenían que pasar la pelota por un círculo. Las mujeres y los niños jugaban mucho.

4. Los incas vivían al oeste de Sudamérica. Dos de sus ciudades famosas son Cuzco y Machu Pichu.

5. Hernán Cortés conquistó los aztecas y Francisco Pizarro conquistó los incas.

Presentation Suggestion:

Allow students to work with a partner on this activity. Ask each student to take a moment to read the statements and think about whether they are true or false. Then have the students discuss their answers with a partner. Encourage students to share what they know about the Aztecs, Incas, and Mayas with their partner. Students also should ask each other questions and challenge their partners' ideas.

Solution:

1. Verdadero.

2. Falso—the Aztecs were not ruled by presidents. One of the most famous Aztec rulers was Moctezuma. Francisco Vásquez de Coronado was a Spanish explorer who traveled what is now known as Arizona and New Mexico.

3. Falso—Mayans did play a ball game. However, the game was very serious (losing often resulted in death!) and women and children were not allowed to play.

4. Verdadero.

5. Verdadero.

Standards Targeted: 1.1, 1.2, 1.3, and 3.1

112. Algo en común – las ciencias sociales

Versión 1:	Versión 2:
Las cosas en los siguientes grupos tienen algo en común. Tienes que averiguar que tienen en común.	The items in each of the following sets share something in common. You have to find out what they have in common.

Versión 1:

ejemplo: Moctezuma • Cuauhtemoc • Huitzilihuitl

respuesta: emperadores aztecas

1. Managua • Montevideo • Asunción • Lima

2. de la Plata • Amazonas • Grande • Negro

3. Felipe Calderón • Benito Juárez • Porfirio Díaz • Vicente Fox

4. Don Juan Carlos • Doña Sofia• la Infanta Elena • la Infanta Cristina • Don Felipe

Versión 2:

ejemplo: Moctezuma • Cuauhtemoc • Huitzilihuitl

answer: Aztec emperors

1. Managua • Montevideo • Asunción • Lima

2. de la Plata • Amazonas • Grande • Negro

3. Felipe Calderón • Benito Juárez • Porfirio Díaz • Vicente Fox

4. Don Juan Carlos • Doña Sofia• la Infanta Elena • la Infanta Cristina • Don Felipe

Presentation Suggestion:

If students have access to computers, this can be an interesting activity to complete using the Internet. Encourage students to use the Internet to learn about the items on each list and discover how they are connected.

This activity can also be a fun group exercise. Have each student from a group look up one item from the list. Then, students should share information with each other. As they listen to each other and share their research they will discover together how the items are connected.

Solution:

1. Capitales (Managua, Nicaragua; Montevideo, Uruguay; Asunción, Paraguay; Lima, Perú)

2. Ríos

3. Presidentes de México

4. Miembros de la familia real española

Standards Targeted: 1.1, 1.2, 1.3, 3.1, and 3.2

113. Cambiando dinero I

Preparation:

The activity found on the next page can be photocopied, displayed on a projector, or copied onto a chalkboard/whiteboard. Select the method that works best for your classroom.

Presentation Suggestion:

Although these exchange rates were accurate at publication time, you may want to look up the current exchange rates as they change daily. Modify the exchange rates as appropriate.

Although this activity fits well with clothing vocabulary, it can easily be modified to fit with the vocabulary you are studying or need to review. Change the exercise so that it includes appropriate vocabulary for your students.

Many students erroneously believe that when they exchange currencies they are making or losing money. Therefore, when they look at this exercise they may initially say that everything is cheapest at Estilo because that is where the numbers are smallest. Encourage students to use the exchange rates to compare the prices in one common currency (they can use U.S. dollars or convert all the currencies into one of the three that are listed). Students should only compare prices using one currency.

Additional Information:

In most Spanish-speaking countries, the comma is used to show a decimal and the period is used to show thousands. However, for this exercise, the comma and period are used in the way they are traditionally used in the United States. If your students are familiar with how numbers are written internationally, you may want to modify the problem accordingly.

Solution:

1. The shoes are least expensive at Tienda Marta ($20).
2. The belt is least expensive at SuperModa ($5).
3. The jacket is least expensive at Estilo ($70).

Standards Targeted: 1.1, 1.2, 1.3, 3.1, and 3.2

Cambiando dinero I (versión 1)

Estás haciendo unas compras en la Red. Tienes que comparar los precios en varias tiendas pero las tiendas están en diferentes países; entonces, tienes que comparar monedas diferentes. Averigua que tienda tiene el mejor precio para cada artículo.

Las tiendas:

SuperModa en Venezuela
$1 = 2,150 bolívares
Estilo en Perú
$1 = 3.25 nuevos soles
Tienda Marta en Chile
$1 = 590 pesos chilenos

2. Un cinturón cuesta...

10,750 en SuperModa

22.75 en Estilo

5,310 en Tienda Marta

¿Dónde compras tu cinturón?

1. Zapatos cuestan...

53,750 en SuperModa

162.50 en Estilo

11,800 en Tienda Marta

¿Dónde compras tus zapatos?

3. Una chaqueta cuesta...

161,250 en SuperModa

227.50 en Estilo

53,100 en Tienda Marta

¿Dónde compras tu chaqueta?

Cambiando dinero I (versión 2)

You are making some purchases on the Internet. You need to compare prices at various stores but the stores are in different countries; therefore, you need to compare different currencies. Find out which store has the best price for each item.

Las tiendas:

SuperModa en Venezuela
$1 = 2,150 bolívares
Estilo en Perú
$1 = 3.25 nuevos soles
Tienda Marta en Chile
$1 = 590 pesos chilenos

2. Un cinturón cuesta...

10,750 en SuperModa

22.75 en Estilo

5,310 en Tienda Marta

¿Dónde compras tu cinturón?

1. Zapatos cuestan...

53,750 en SuperModa

162.50 en Estilo

11,800 en Tienda Marta

¿Dónde compras tus zapatos?

3. Una chaqueta cuesta...

161,250 en SuperModa

227.50 en Estilo

53,100 en Tienda Marta

¿Dónde compras tu chaqueta?

114. Cambiando dinero II

Versión 1:

Cuando viajas o haces compras internacionales es importante saber cambiar dinero. Practica con los siguientes problemas.

Ejemplo:

$1 = 0.78 euros

Si cambias $5 a euros ¿cuánto tienes?

$5 \times 0.78 = 3.90$ euros

Si cambias 5 euros a dólares ¿cuánto tienes?

$5 \div 0.78 = \$6.41$

$1 = 561 colones

1. Si cambias $2 a colones ¿cuánto tienes?

2. Si cambias 3927 colones a dólares ¿cuánto tienes?

$1 = 14.41 pesos mexicanos

3. Si cambias $15 a pesos ¿cuánto tienes?

4. Si cambias 158.51 pesos a dólares ¿cuánto tienes?

Versión 2:

When you travel or make international purchases, it is important to know how to exchange money. Practice with the following problems.

Ejemplo:

$1 = 0.78 euros

Si cambias $5 a euros ¿cuánto tienes?

$5 \times 0.78 = 3.90$ euros

Si cambias 5 euros a dólares ¿cuánto tienes?

$5 \div 0.78 = \$6.41$

$1 = 561 colones

1. Si cambias $2 a colones ¿cuánto tienes?

2. Si cambias 3927 colones a dólares ¿cuánto tienes?

$1 = 14.41 pesos mexicanos

3. Si cambias $15 a pesos ¿cuánto tienes?

4. Si cambias 158.51 pesos a dólares ¿cuánto tienes?

Presentation Suggestion:

Although these exchange rates were accurate at writing time, you may want to look up the current exchange rates as they change daily. Modify this exercise to include current exchange rates.

Additional Information:

In most Spanish-speaking countries, the comma is used to show a decimal and the period is used to show thousands. However, for this exercise, the comma and period are used in the way they are traditionally used in the United States. If your students are familiar with how numbers are written internationally, you may want to modify the problem accordingly.

Solution:

1. 1122 colones
2. $7
3. 216.15 pesos
4. $11

Standards Targeted: 1.1, 1.2, 1.3, 3.1, and 3.2

115. Cambiando dinero III

En muchos lugares donde hay turistas, puedes pagar con dinero local o usar dólares americanos. A veces turistas piensan que no importa si usan dólares o el dinero local. ¡Pero hay que tener cuidado! Muchas veces si pagas en dólares cuesta más. Mira el siguiente menú de un restaurante en Guatemala. Tiene precios en dólares y en quetzales. ¿Para cada comida es una buena idea pagar en dólares o debes usar quetzales?

$1 = 8 quetzales

Menú:

Bebidas:
Agua: 13 quetzales ($1)
Refresco: 16 quetzales ($2)
Licuado: 15 quetzales ($2)

Comida:
Empanada: 35 quetzales ($4)
Tamale: 20 quetzales ($3)
Tacos: 25 quetzales ($4)

You can pay with the local currency or use dollars at many tourist locations overseas. Sometimes tourists think that it doesn't matter if they use dollars or the local currency. However, you have to be very careful! Sometimes you will be charged more if you pay in dollars. Look at the following menu for a restaurant in Guatemala. It has prices in dollars and quetzales. For each item, is it a good idea to use dollars or should you pay with quetzales?

$1 = 8 quetzales

Menú:

Bebidas:
Agua: 13 quetzales ($1)
Refresco: 16 quetzales ($2)
Licuado: 15 quetzales ($2)

Comida:
Empanada: 35 quetzales ($4)
Tamale: 20 quetzales ($3)
Tacos: 25 quetzales ($4)

Additional Information:

In general, it is best to use the local currency when traveling overseas. Stores and restaurants often charge their customers substantially more if they use dollars. Even stores that use the current exchange rate will usually round up to the nearest dollar instead of dealing with change. Furthermore, there are sometimes extra fees for using dollars. Students should be aware, however, that there may be a few items (such as the water and empanadas in this exercise) that are cheaper in dollars.

Solution:

Agua	13 quetzales ($1)	Better to use dollars
Refresco	16 quetzales ($2)	The same price in dollars and quetzales
Licuado	15 quetzales ($2)	Better to use quetzales
Empanada	35 quetzales ($4)	Better to use dollars
Tamale	20 quetzales ($3)	Better to use quetzales
Tacos	25 quetzales ($4)	Better to use quetzales

Standards Targeted: 1.1, 1.2, 1.3, 3.1, and 3.2

116. ¿Qué hora es?

Preparation:

You will need to give students copies of a time-zone map.

Versión 1:	Versión 2:
Cuando viajas tienes que prestar atención a los cambios de hora. Usa un mapa de las horas internacionales para responder a las preguntas.	When traveling, you often have to pay close attention to time changes. Use a time zone map to answer the questions.

Versión 1:

Cuando viajas tienes que prestar atención a los cambios de hora. Usa un mapa de las horas internacionales para responder a las preguntas.

1. María está de viaje en Montevideo, Uruguay. Ella quiere llamar a su mamá en Los Ángeles. ¿A qué hora debe María llamar de Montevideo para hablar con su mamá a las cinco en Los Ángeles?

2. Samuel vive en Alaska y tiene un amigo (Marcos) que vive in México. En su clase de español quieren llamar a Marcos. La clase de español es a las 10 de la mañana en Alaska. ¿Qué hora es en México?

3. Liliana vuela de Chicago a Madrid. El vuelo dura 8 horas. Ella sale de Chicago a las 5 de la tarde. ¿A qué hora llega a Madrid en tiempo local?

Versión 2:

When traveling, you often have to pay close attention to time changes. Use a time zone map to answer the questions.

1. Maria is on a trip in Montevideo, Uruguay. She wants to call her mom who lives in Los Angeles. What time should Maria call from Montevideo if she wants it to be 5:00 P.M. in Los Angeles?

2. Samuel lives in Alaska and his friend, Marcos, lives in Mexico. Samuel's Spanish class wants to call Marcos. The Spanish class starts at 10 A.M. in Alaska. What time would that be in Mexico?

3. Liliana is flying from Chicago to Madrid. The flight takes 8 hours. She leaves Chicago at 5 P.M. What time will it be when she arrives in Madrid? (Give your answer in local time.)

Presentation Suggestion:

If students have never worked with a time zone map, they may need instruction on how to use the map. Many textbooks include a world time zone map and you can direct students to the correct page. If not, you will need to copy one for your students to use on this problem.

Solution:

1. It would be 10 P.M. in Montevideo.
2. It would be 1 P.M. in Mexico.
3. She arrives at 8 A.M. local time.

Standards Targeted: 1.1, 1.2, 1.3, 3.1, and 3.2

117. ¿Qué hora es? II

Preparation:
You will need to give students copies of a time-zone map.

Versión 1:	Versión 2:
Muchas veces las impresas internacionales tienen que tener reuniones usando el teléfono o un sistema de video. Arreglar estas reuniones puede ser muy complicado cuando las personas están en diferentes partes del mundo y hay una diferencia horaria. Mira un mapa de las horas internacionales y averigua cuándo las siguientes personas deben planear una reunión. Explica por qué escogiste esa hora.	International companies often have to schedule phone meetings or video conferences. However, scheduling these meetings becomes even more complicated when you need to cross multiple time zones. Look at a time zone map and try to find the best time for the following people to schedule a meeting (via the phone or video). Explain why you selected that time.

Versión 1:

1. Pablo en Madrid, España
   María en La Paz, Bolivia
   Carlos en Santiago, Chile
2. Sara en San Juan, Puerto Rico
   Ester en New York, EEUU
   José en Managua, Nicaragua
3. Paco en San Salvador, El Salvador
   Luisa en París, Francia
   Jorge en Moscú, Rusia
   Carina en Tokio, Japón

Versión 2:

1. Pablo en Madrid, España
   María en La Paz, Bolivia
   Carlos en Santiago, Chile
2. Sara en San Juan, Puerto Rico
   Ester en New York, EEUU
   José en Managua, Nicaragua
3. Paco en San Salvador, El Salvador
   Luisa en París, Francia
   Jorge en Moscú, Rusia
   Carina en Tokio, Japón

Solution:

Answers will vary. Some *possible answers* include:

1. Pablo in Madrid, Spain – 2 P.M.   María in La Paz, Bolivia – 9 A.M.
   Carlos in Santiago, Chile – 10 A.M.
2. Sara in San Juan – 11 A.M.   Ester in New York, USA – 10 A.M.
   José in Managua, Nicaragua – 9 A.M.
3. There is no perfect solution to this problem. When scheduling international meetings, people often need to work at different times. A possible solution is:
   Paco in San Salvador, El Salvador – 6 A.M.
   Luisa in Paris, France – 1 P.M.
   Jorge in Moscow, Russia – 3 P.M.
   Carina in Tokio, Japan – 9 P.M.

Standards Targeted: 1.1, 1.2, 1.3, 3.1, and 3.2

118. Números maya: 0-20

Versión 1:

Los Maya tenían un sistema de matemáticas muy interesante. Usaron conchas, puntos y líneas para mostrar los números. Una concha vale cero, un punto vale uno, y una línea es cinco. Mira los siguientes ejemplos.

= 0

= 3

= 6

= 19

Ahora intenta escribir los siguientes números usando el sistema maya.

2, 8, 10, 13, 16

Intenta adivinar como representan el número 20.

Versión 2:

The Maya had an interesting system of mathematics. They used shells, dots, and lines to show numbers. A shell represents zero, a dot is one, and a line is five. Look at the following examples.

= 0

= 3

= 6

= 19

Now try to write the following numbers out using the Mayan system.

2, 8, 10, 13, 16

Try to guess how they would represent 20.

Additional Information:

When Mayan merchants were doing calculations for sales, they often used cocoa beans for the dots. Many people believe that the system consists of fives and twenties because there are five fingers on your hand and twenty fingers and toes combined. This system is base twenty (vigesimal) although the number system we use is base ten.

Solution:

= 2   = 8   =10

= 13   =16   =20

Standards Targeted: 1.1, 1.2, 1.3, 3.1, and 3.2

119. Números maya: números grandes

Preparation:

Copy the appropriate student handout (versión 1 or 2). If you prefer, copy the appropriate information onto an overhead transparency or display on a projector.

Presentation Suggestion:

This problem builds on the information from #118 and should be presented sequentially. The challenge question requires students to take their understanding and apply it to a new row (the third row). Encourage students to think about how they could solve the problem and then have all the students at least provide their best hypothesis.

Consider allowing students to work with partners on this activity. Some students may find it challenging to think about a number system that is a base twenty system. Working with a peer may help students understand the new system.

Additional Information:

As a base twenty system, each additional row is a power of twenty. The bottom row represents the ones, the second row is the twenties, the third row is the 400s and the fourth row is the 8000s.

Variations and Additional Activities:

Encourage students to challenge each other. Have students write numbers using the Mayan system and then trade papers with a partner. Their partners should then write the numbers using our numerical system.

Solution:

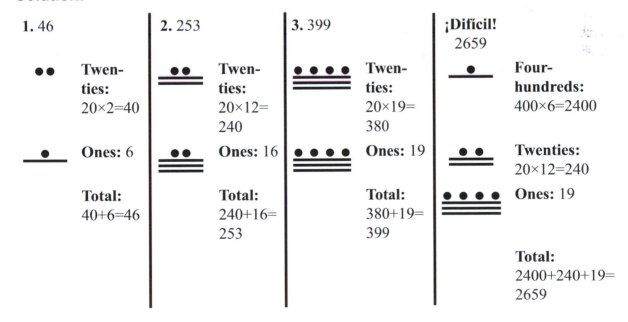

Standards Targeted: 1.1, 1.2, 1.3, 3.1, and 3.2

Números maya: números grandes (versión 1)

Ayer aprendiste a escribir los números hasta 20 usando el sistema maya. Cuando llegas a 20, usas diferentes filas. La primera fila representa el número de veintes y la segunda fila representa los números hasta 20.

ejemplos:

Vientes: Hay 3 veintes o 60 (3 × 20)

Unidades: Hay 7

Total: 67

Veintes: Como hay 9 son 180 (9 × 20)

Unidades: Solo hay 1

Total: 181

Mira los siguientes números maya. Puedes escribirlos usando nuestro sistema?

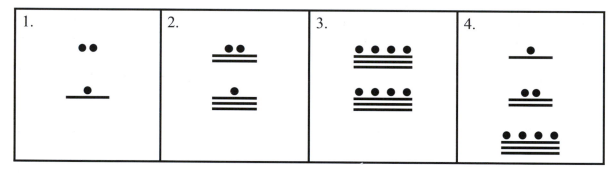

Yesterday you learned how to write numbers up to twenty using the Mayan numbering system. Once you get past twenty, you create rows. The top row represents the number of twenties and the second row represents the ones.

examples:

● ● ●   **Twenties row:** Since there are 3 this represents 60 (3 × 20)

● ●   **Ones row:** There are 7 here
─────

Total: 67

● ● ● ●   **Twenties row:** Since there are 9 this represents 180 (9 × 20)

●   **Ones row:** There is 1 here

Total: 181

Look at the following Mayan numbers. Can you write them out using our system?

1.	2.	3.	4.
● ● ● ───	● ● ═══ ● ═══	● ● ● ● ═══ ● ● ● ● ═══	● ─── ● ● ═══ ● ● ● ● ═══

120. Números maya: sumas y restas

Preparation:
Copy the appropriate student handout (versión 1or 2). If you prefer, copy the appropriate information onto an overhead transparency or display on a projector.

Presentation Suggestion:
This problem builds on the information from #118 and #119 and should be presented sequentially.

Variations and Additional Activities:
Have students write their own problems using Mayan numbers or our numerical system. Then, have them trade papers with a partner and either solve the problems or translate the numbers between the two systems.

Solution:

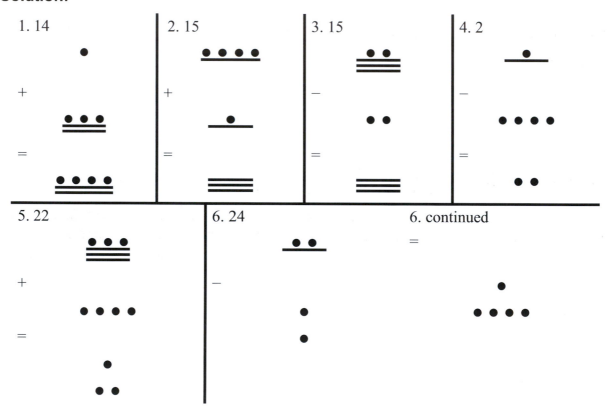

Standards Targeted: 1.1, 1.2, 1.3, 3.1, and 3.2

Ahora casi eres un experto en los números maya. Hoy vas a usar los números para hacer sumas y restas (es bastante simple con este sistema). No te olvides de que cinco puntos hacen una línea. Si no tienes suficientes puntos para una resta, cambia una línea a cinco puntos.

ejemplos:

$$6 + 7 = 13$$

$$19 - 12 = 7$$

Ahora, escribe los siguientes problemas usando números Mayas y escribe la solución.

1. $1 + 13 =$
2. $9 + 6 =$
3. $17 - 2 =$
4. $6 - 4 =$

Más difícil:

5. $18 + 4 =$
6. $45 - 21 =$

Números maya: sumas y restas (versión 2)

You are now almost an expert in Mayan numbers. Today, you are going to use the numbers to add and subtract (which is basically very simple). Remember that if you have five dots they become a line. With subtraction, if you don't have enough dots, change a line into five dots.

examples:

$$6 + 7 = 13$$

$$19 - 12 = 7$$

Write out the following problems using Mayan numbers and then solve.

1. $1 + 13 =$
2. $9 + 6 =$
3. $17 - 2 =$
4. $6 - 4 =$

Más difícil:

5. $18 + 4 =$
6. $45 - 21 =$

121. El sistema métrico

Versión 1:	Versión 2:
La mayoría del mundo usa el sistema métrico. Incluso en los Estados Unidos muchos profesionales normalmente usan el sistema métrico (como los doctores o científicos). Entonces, es importante tener un conocimiento básico del sistema métrico.	In most of the world people use the metric system. Even in the United States a lot of professionals use the metric system (such as doctors and scientists). Therefore, it is important to have some basic knowledge of this system.
Escribe aproximadamente cuánto son estas cantidades usando el sistema americano. Si no sabes, puedes adivinar.	For each of the following quantities, write their equivalents using the American system. If you don't know, write down your best guess.
1. Un centímetro	1. Un centímetro
2. Un metro	2. Un metro
3. Un kilómetro	3. Un kilómetro
4. Un gramo	4. Un gramo
5. Un kilogramo	5. Un kilogramo
6. Un mililitro	6. Un mililitro
7. Un litro	7. Un litro

Presentation Suggestion:

If time permits you may want to explain to students that the metric system is based on tens. Encourage students to think about what the prefixes "centi," "kilo," and "mili" mean.

You may also want to help students think of real-life examples for what each unit represents (e.g., a paperclip or a dime each weighs about 1 gram). If students are going to begin using the metric system, it is important for them to understand what each unit represents.

Solution:

Students answers may vary if they estimated with a different American unit.
1. Un centímetro = 0.39 pulgadas (inches)
2. Un metro = 1.09 yardas (yards) o 3.28 pies (feet)
3. Un kilómetro = 0.62 millas (miles)
4. Un gramo = 0.035 onzas (ounces)
5. Un kilogramo = 2.2 libras (pounds)
6. Un mililitro = 0.2 cucharitas (teaspoons)
7. Un litro = 0.264 galones (gallons)

Standards Targeted: 1.1, 1.2, 1.3, 3.1, and 3.2

122. El sistema métrico II

Versión 1:	Versión 2:
En los Estados Unidos hay una semana oficial dedicada al sistema métrico. La semana siempre incluye el 10 de octubre (o 10/10). ¿Por qué tiene sentido celebrar el sistema métrico el 10 de octubre?	There is actually an official metric week in the United states. The week always includes the tenth of October (or 10/10). Why does it make sense to celebrate the metric system on the tenth of October?
Muchos estadounidenses quieren adoptar el sistema métrico. ¿En tu opinión es una buena idea? ¿Cuáles son las ventajas y las desventajas de cambiar al sistema métrico?	Many people in the United States want to adopt the metric system. In your opinion, is this a good idea? What are the advantages and disadvantages of adopting the metric system?

Presentation Suggestion:

If possible, present this exercise and the one before it during metric week! You can also do other activities in class to celebrate metric week. For more information you may want to browse the U.S. Metric Association's website or visit other sites.

Solution:

Students' answers will vary. October 10 is a good fit for metric week as its date is 10/10 and the metric system is based entirely on groups of ten. Some advantages and disadvantages of adopting the metric system include:

Advantages:	Disadvantages:
♦ It facilitates international trade and communication since everyone is using the same system of measurement. Only three countries currently do not use the metric system.	♦ Transitioning to a new system is expensive (you have to print new materials such as road signs).
♦ Because the metric system is based on groups of ten, it is easier to learn and use.	♦ The United States customary system is too infused in our culture (a football field is measured in yards, our races are measured in miles, our milk is sold in gallons, hardware and machinery are built to conform to English measurements, etc.)
♦ Every year there are conversion mistakes made as doctors and other professionals use the metric system but patients and other consumers do not.	
♦ Many products are produced internationally and actually based on metric measurements (such as two-liter bottles). It makes sense to use the same measurements around the world.	♦ People who grew up using the United States customary system of inches and pounds would need to learn to correctly use the metric system.

Standards Targeted: 1.1, 1.2, 1.3, 3.1, and 3.2

123. Protegiendo nuestra tierra

Versión 1:	Versión 2:
Muchas personas piensan que debemos hacer más para proteger nuestro medio ambiente. ¿Cuáles son algunas cosas que nosotros podemos hacer para proteger nuestra tierra?	Protecting our environment is a concern for many people. What are some things that we can do to protect our environment? Try to write as much in Spanish as possible.

Solution:

Student answers will vary. Encourage students to think about things that they can do on a regular basis to reduce, reuse, and recycle. This can also be a great opportunity to talk with your students about the need for international cooperation and efforts. Also, remind students that Spanish is an important language for the international scientific community!

Additional Information:

In the United States, Earth Day is celebrated on April 22. Consider doing this activity on or around April 22 to encourage students to think about how we can protect the environment. Earth day is celebrated around the world. However, in the southern hemisphere many countries celebrate in the fall.

Standards Targeted: 1.1, 1.2, 1.3, 3.1, and 3.2

124. Las aves migratorias

Versión 1:	Versión 2:
¿Te gustaría viajar del norte de Canadá hasta el sur extremo de Sudamérica cada año? ¡Muchos pájaros lo hacen! Las aves migratorias vuelan a diferentes partes del mundo cuando el clima cambia. El playero gordo (*Calidris canutus*) es un ejemplo de un pájaro que viaja casi 32.000 kilómetros (20,000 miles) en un año. Los científicos que estudian estos pájaros también viajan mucho. Saber hablar otro idioma puede ser muy importante para los científicos cuando viajan a otros países y trabajan con científicos locales. ¿Cuáles son algunos de los problemas en proteger aves (especialmente aves que viajan gran distancias)?	Would you like to travel from the northern part of Canada to the southernmost part of South America every year? Many birds do just this. Migratory birds travel to different places around the world following warm weather. The Red knot (*Calidris canutus*) is an example of a bird that travels almost 20,000 miles (or 32,000 kilometers) every year. Scientists who study these birds often also travel extensively. Speaking another language can be very beneficial for these scientists as they travel to other countries and work with local scientists. What are some of the challenges in protecting birds (especially birds that travel these great distances)?

Solution:

Protecting migratory birds requires extensive collaboration between different countries. A change in fertilizers, hunting, or pollution in one country can disrupt the migratory pattern of these birds. Furthermore, if the birds cannot complete their voyage, they can die. If a population of birds decreases, this can disrupt the ecosystem tremendously (e.g., the insects that the birds used to eat might increase dramatically in population). It is critical that different people work together to protect the world's natural habitat and species. Learning another language can be a huge asset for international scientists.

Standards Targeted: 1.1, 1.2, 1.3, 3.1, 3.2, and 5.1

125. La ciencia de cocinar

Versión 1:	Versión 2:
Si analizas la comida típica de un país puedes aprender mucho sobre el país y su clima. Lee las siguientes descripciones de comidas típicas. Usando esta información intenta adivinar el clima de la región y de qué país viene cada comida.	Traditional dishes can tell you a lot about a country and its climate. Read through the following traditional dishes. Then, guess what the climate must be like in that area and where that food might be from.
Paella con mariscos: arroz, calamares, camarones, almejas, aceite, tomate, azafrán, pimentón, cebolla, y sal	**Paella con mariscos:** rice, squid, shrimp, clams, oil, tomato, saffron, pepper, onion, and salt
Gallo pinto: arroz, frijoles, cebolla, pimentón, cilantro, huevos, natilla, y plátano frito	**Gallo pinto:** rice, black beans, onion, pepper, cilantro, eggs, sour cream, and fried plantain
Asado: variedad de carnes asados, empanadas, y ensalada	**Asado:** variety of grilled meats, empanadas (pastry filled with meat or cheese), and salad

Solution:

Paella con mariscos is a traditional dish from Spain. It is commonly served on coastal regions where there is a lot of access to seafood. Because Spain is a peninsula, many regions have access to a constant supply of seafood.

Gallo pinto is a traditional dish from Costa Rica. Costa Rica's tropical climate is well-suited for growing plantains, beans, and rice.

Asado is a traditional meal from Argentina (for the purpose of this exercise other sides are included although they are not necessarily part of eating grilled meat). Argentina is well-known for its cattle industry. The "pampas," a large, fertile area filled with grasses and vegetation, are an ideal place for cattle to grow and feed.

Variations and Additional Activities:

Modify the activity to include food from countries you have recently studied or are planning to feature in upcoming lessons. Also, encourage students to think of typical foods from other countries and then relate the food to the climate and natural resources for that country.

Standards Targeted: 1.1, 1.2, 1.3, 2.1, 2.2, and 3.1

126. Los nombres de los huracanes

Versión 1:	Versión 2:

Versión 1:

¿Sabes cómo reciben los huracanes sus nombres? La Organización Meteorológica Mundial tiene una lista de nombres para cada letra del alfabeto (omitiendo la Q, U, X, Y, y Z). Cada año las tormentas tropicales fuertes reciben nombres en orden alfabético. Por ejemplo, la primera tormenta de un año podría ser "Adán" y la segunda tormenta podría ser "Beatriz." Si una tormenta causa muchas muertes generalmente retiran el nombre de la lista.

1. ¿Por qué crees que no incluyen Q, U, X, Y, y Z en la lista de nombres?

2. ¿Qué nombre podría venir después de "Gabriel?"

3. Imagina que hay 4 tormentas fuertes en agosto. ¿Si la última tormenta se llama "Timoteo" cuál sería un nombre posible para la primera tormenta?

Versión 2:

Do you know how hurricanes are named? The World Meteorological Organization has a list of names for every letter of the alphabet (they omit Q, U, X, Y, and Z). Severe tropical storms are named alphabetically. For example, the first storm of a year may be named "Adam" and the second storm could be "Beatriz." The names for storms that cause many deaths are usually removed from the list.

1. Why do you think the letters Q, U, X, Y, and Z are omitted from the list?

2. What name could come after "Gabriel?"

3. If there are four storms in August and the last one is named "Timoteo" what might the first one have been named?

Solution:

1. Those letters are omitted because there aren't enough names that begin with those letters.
2. Answers will vary but should begin with the letter "H."
3. Answers will vary but should begin with the letter "P."

Variations and Additional Activities:

Ask students to track severe storms for a month or two and follow the naming patterns. If very severe weather causes damage to an area, ask students to think about how the international community can and does help people facing natural disasters. Encourage students to think about how learning another language can help them in the field of international service.

Standards Targeted: 1.1, 1.2, 1.3, and 3.1

Otros idiomas

Activities that teach about language origins
and connections between languages

127. ¿Cuánto sabes sobre el español?

Versión 1:	Versión 2:
Responde a las siguientes preguntas para ver cuánto sabes sobre el español.	Answer the following questions to see how much you know about Spanish.

Versión 1:

Responde a las siguientes preguntas para ver cuánto sabes sobre el español.

1. Verdadero o falso: En inglés dicen que el español es un lenguaje "Romance" porque viene del latín.

2. El español tiene influencia árabe. ¿Por qué?

3. Las Naciones Unidas tiene 6 idiomas oficiales. ¿Es el español un idioma oficial para las Naciones Unidas? ¿Puedes escribir una lista con los 6 idiomas?

4. Verdadero o falso: Hay aproximadamente 1 millón de hispanohablantes en el mundo.

Versión 2:

Answer the following questions to see how much you know about Spanish.

1. True or False: Spanish is a Romance language, meaning it comes from Latin.

2. Spanish is influenced by Arabic. Why?

3. There are six official languages for the United Nations. Is Spanish one of them? Can you name all six?

4. True or False: About 1 million people speak Spanish.

Presentation Suggestion:

Modify the statements based on your students' knowledge and your curricular goals. Ask more advanced students to explain why they believe statements are true or false.

Solution:

1. True. Students often wonder, "What makes Spanish romantic and not English?" Encourage students to hypothesize why a language would be called a "Romance language." You may need to remind them that the *Romans* once controlled much of Europe.

2. The Moors ruled Spain from 711 to 1492. During this time, Arabic, the language of the Moors, infiltrated Spanish and that influence remains today.

3. Yes. The six languages are Spanish, Chinese, English, French, Russian, and Arabic.

4. False. Current estimates are that almost half a billion people speak Spanish worldwide.

Standards Targeted: 1.1, 1.2, 1.3, 3.1, and 3.2

128. La influencia árabe

Versión 1:	Versión 2:
Como los moros controlaron España por casi 800 años, muchas palabras españolas vienen del árabe. Lee las siguientes palabras en árabe e intenta adivinar cómo decir las palabras en español e inglés.	Since the Moors ruled Spain for almost 800 years, many Spanish words come from Arabic. Read the following Arabic words and see if you can guess what they are in Spanish and English.
1. azzaytúna	1. azzaytúna
2. aššiṭranğ	2. aššiṭranğ
3. alḥabáqa	3. alḥabáqa
4. alḫaršúf[a]	4. alḫaršúf[a]
5. alqáḍi	5. alqáḍi
6. alfáṣfaṣ	6. alfáṣfaṣ
7. alquṭún	7. alquṭún
8. almuḫádda	8. almuḫádda
9. assúkkar	9. assúkkar
10. arráwz	10. arráwz

Presentation Suggestion:

You may want to give students three or four minutes to try and identify what the words could mean in Spanish. Then, you could allow students to work in small groups and/or provide the students with some hints, such as "Puedes comer números 1, 3, 4, 6, 9 and 10."

Solution:

1. azzaytúna	aceituna (olive)		6. alfáṣfaṣ	alfalfa (alfalfa)
2. aššiṭranğ	ajedrez (chess)		7. alquṭún	algodón (cotton)
3. alḥabáqa	albahaca (basil)		8. almuḫádda	almohada (pillow)
4. alḫaršúf[a]	alcachofa (artichoke)		9. assúkkar	azúcar (sugar)
5. alqáḍi	alcalde (mayor)		10. arráwz	arroz (rice)

Standards Targeted: 1.1, 1.2, 1.3, 3.1, 3.2, and 4.1

129. La influencia francesa

Versión 1:	Versión 2:
El español tiene muchas palabras de origen francés. Haz una línea conectando las correspondientes palabras en español, francés e inglés.	Spanish has a number of words of French origin. Draw a line connecting the matching Spanish, French and English words.

español:		francés:		inglés:	
frambuesa	gabinete	sofa	blouse	hotel	sofa
gripe	hotel	gabinet	bébé	truck	pants
bebé	pantalón	pantalon	silhou-	flu	cabinet
blusa	silueta	framboise	ette	raspberry	blouse
camión	sofá	grippe	hôtel	baby	silhouette
			camion		

Presentation Suggestion:

Students could either copy the chart from the board/overhead or you could provide students with copies of this activity. Alternately, you could put all the words in a bank.

Many students erroneously believe that if a word in any other language sounds like an English word, then the other language must come from English. Call to students attention that many of the English words from the list above come from French just like the Spanish words come from French.

If you have students who speak French in your class, encourage them to share additional words that come from French. Students could also identify words in Spanish and French that are cognates.

Solution:

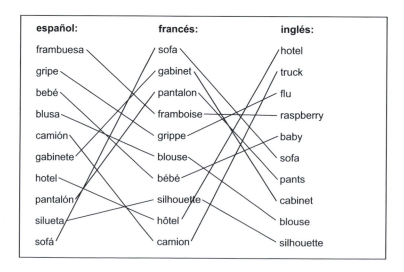

Standards Targeted:

130. La influencia amerindia

Versión 1:	Versión 2:
Mira la siguiente lista de palabras y busca las palabras con el mismo significado en español, inglés y lengua amerindia. Al final debes tener 10 grupos de palabras.	From the following bank of words, try to match up the Spanish, English, and Native American words that have the same meaning. You should have 10 sets of words.

Lista de palabras:

chilli mahís
jicama chile chicle ahuacatl
tomatl corn
tapioca guacamole aguacate
tzictli gum tomato
cacao
cacao maíz chocolate xocoatl tapioca
xicamatl
tomate tipiog chocolate
ahuacamulli cacáhuatl
guacamole chili jícama
aguacate avocado

Presentation Suggestion:

Consider putting the word bank on a chalkboard or copy the bank onto an overhead sheet. However, some students will find it difficult to look up at the board and then down at their papers repeatedly. Instead, you could make photocopies of the word bank for all students.

To simplify the problem you can write the Spanish words in one color, the English words in another, and the American Indian words in another color. However, by mixing the words you can see which students understand the rules for Spanish spelling. Students should be able to accurately pick out most of the Spanish words even if they have not seen them before. If students struggle with this, you could use this as an opportunity to review Spanish spelling rules.

Solution:

Español:		Inglés:		Lengua amerindia:	
aguacate	maíz	avocado	corn	ahuacatl (nahua)	mahís (taíno)
cacao	tomate	cacao	tomato	cacáhuatl (nahua)	tomatl (nahua)
chicle	tapioca	gum	tapioca	tzictli (nahua)	tipiog (guaraní)
chocolate	jícama	chocolate	jicama	xocoatl (nahua)	xicamatl (na-hua)
guacamole	chile	guaca-mole	chili	ahuacamulli (na-hua)	chilli (nahua)

Standards Targeted: 1.1, 1.2, 1.3, 3.1, 3.2, and 4.1

131. Conexiones con muchos idiomas

Preparation:

Make copies of the following student handout. You could display it on an overhead or LCD projector if you prefer.

Variations and Additional Activities:

Encourage students to constantly investigate languages and look for connections between languages. If any of your students speak other languages, ask them to share what connections they see between Spanish and the other languages they speak (or are studying). When students are learning new vocabulary words in English, ask them to think about how Spanish can help them increase their English vocabulary.

Consider creating a bulletin board or other location to display information about connections between different languages. Throughout the semester or year, students can add new words that they learn. Also, encourage students to do research on where different words come originated.

Solution:

Palabra en español	Idioma de origen	Palabra en ese idioma	Palabra en inglés
Canguro	Guugu Yimidhirr (en Australia)	Gangurru	Kangaroo
Charlar	Italiano	Ciarlare	To talk
Espía	Alemán gótico	Spaíha	Spy
Guerra	Alemán	Werra	War
Mermelada	Portugués	Marmelada	Marmalade/Jam
Música	Griego	μουσική	Music
Poema	Griego	ποίημα	Poem
Quimono	Japonés	Kimono	Kimono
Trampolín	Italiano	Trampolino	Trampoline
Volcán	Portugués	Volcão	Volcano

Standards Targeted: 1.1, 1.2, 1.3, 3.1, 3.2, and 4.1

Conexiones con muchos idiomas (versión 1)

El español ha tomado palabras de muchos idiomas, aunque de algunos idiomas ha tomado muy pocas palabras. Intenta completar la siguiente tabla con 10 palabras de otros idiomas.

Palabra en español	Idioma de origen	Palabra en ese idioma	Palabra en inglés
	Guugu Yimidhirr (en Australia)	Gangurru	
Charlar		Ciarlare	
Espía	Alemán gótico	Spaíha	
		Werra	War
Mermelada	Portugués	Marmelada	
Música		μουσική	Music
		ποίημα	Poem
Quimono	Japonés		
	Italiano	Trampolino	Trampoline
	Portugués	Volcão	

Conexiones con muchos idiomas (versión 2)

Spanish has taken words from many different languages, although from some languages it has taken very few words. Try to complete the following table with 10 words with foreign origins.

Palabra en español	Idioma de origen	Palabra en ese idioma	Palabra en inglés
	Guugu Yimidhirr (en Australia)	Gangurru	
Charlar		Ciarlare	
Espía	Alemán gótico	Spaíha	
		Werra	War
Mermelada	Portugués	Marmelada	
Música		μουσική	Music
		ποίημα	Poem
Quimono	Japonés		
	Italiano	Trampolino	Trampoline
	Portugués	Volcão	

Dichos

Exercises that teach students about idioms

Los dichos

The following five exercises feature "dichos" or idiomatic expressions. They are presented in a variety of ways to encourage your students to think critically and creatively about what they might mean. Also, use this time to engage students in discussions about the "dichos."

You may want to do all of these exercises in order, or on a certain day of the week. At the end of the mini-unit, consider reviewing all of the dichos and requiring your students to memorize them. Reward students for using the dichos at appropriate times during class. As always, modify the activities to fit with your curriculum. Some dichos fit naturally with specific topics (e.g., "Costar un ojo de la cara" would go well with a clothing unit). Select dichos that will enhance your curriculum or modify the activities to meet your instructional goals.

132. Tomar el pelo...

Versión 1:	Versión 2:
Un joven compra una pegatina de tatuaje falso. Un día en la escuela se pone el tatuaje antes de regresar a casa. Cuando está cenando con su familia su papá nota el tatuaje y dice, "hijo, ¿qué tienes en el brazo?"	Un joven compra una pegatina de tatuaje falso. Un día en la escuela se pone el tatuaje antes de regresar a casa. Cuando está cenando con su familia su papá nota el tatuaje y dice, "hijo, ¿qué tienes en el brazo?"
El hijo responde, "¿Esto? No es nada, papi. Solo es mi tatuaje nuevo."	El hijo responde, "¿Esto? No es nada, papi. Solo es mi tatuaje nuevo."
El papá empieza a enfadarse pero el hijo respondo, "¡Papi, te tomé el pelo!"	El papá empieza a enfadarse pero el hijo respondo, "¡Papi, te tomé el pelo!"
¿Qué significa el dicho "tomar el pelo?" ¿Cómo se usa en este cuento?	Based on the story, what do you think the expression "tomar el pelo" means?

Presentation Suggestion:

Modify the sample story to best meet your students needs. If students are struggling, consider allowing them to read the story with a partner and discuss what it means. As a followup, ask students to create their own stories or dialogues that feature this expression.

Solution:

"Tomar el pelo" can be used when someone plays a practical joke on another person or when they lie to another person.

Standards Targeted: 1.1, 1.2, 1.3, and 4.1

133. Ser un pez gordo

<table>
<tr><td>

Versión 1:

En español tenemos un dicho para expresar que alguien es muy importante. Usamos "pez gordo" para describir a un jefe o a una persona muy importante. Por ejemplo, si estás hablando con un amigo sobre el trabajo de tu mamá, puedes decir "Hoy mi mamá tiene una reunión con el señor Martínez. Él es un pez gordo en su empresa."

Probablemente no podrías haber adivinado el significado de este dicho. También es posible que pienses que es un poco extraño llamar a un jefe "un pez gordo." Ahora es tu turno para crear un dicho. ¿Qué dicho usarías para describir a un jefe? ¿Puedes crear un dicho sobre otro tópico? ¡Sé creativo!

</td><td>

Versión 2:

In Spanish we have a saying we use to show that someone is very important. We use "pez gordo" (fat fish) to describe a boss or an important person. For example, if you are talking with a friend about your mom's job, you might say, "Hoy mi mamá tiene una reunión con el señor Martínez. Él es un pez gordo en su empresa." ("Today my Mom has a meeting with Mr. Martínez. He is a fat fish at her company.")

You probably couldn't have guessed the meaning of this saying. Also, you might think that it is a little strange to call a boss a "fat fish." Now it is your turn to create your own saying. What expression would you use to describe a boss? Can you create a saying about another topic? Be creative!

</td></tr>
</table>

Presentation Suggestion:

If students finish quickly, suggest that they write a short story like the one above that incorporates their new expression. Then they can read the short story to the class and see if their classmates can guess the meaning of their new saying.

Some students may believe they are creating a new expression when they are actually simply translating one from English (e.g., "una peluca grande" for "big wig"). Encourage students to think creatively and not translate expressions. Also, ask them to defend their new expressions and explain why they make sense.

This task may be difficult for some students to complete quickly. If students have trouble thinking of a new expression in a few minutes, encourage them to continue thinking about it after class. Then, if they come up with a good expression they could share it a few days or even a week later. With more time, students' creativity can really start flowing!

Remind students that new expressions are created every year and incorporated in dictionaries. New sayings often come from popular culture such as music, movies and television. New advances in technology also lead to the creation of new words or expressions (such as "IMing" or "Friending someone."). Once students start thinking about these high-interest topics they can usually come up with some interesting expressions!

Standards Targeted:

1.1, 1.2, 1.3, and 4.1

134. Costar un ojo de la cara

Versión 1:	Versión 2:
Con algunos dichos es difícil adivinar de dónde vienen y que significan. Pero con otros dichos, si piensas en ellos es posible adivinar que significan. Lee el siguiente dicho y escribe lo que piensas que significa. También describe una situación cuando podrías usar este dicho. Costar un ojo de la cara	When you hear some idioms, it is hard to guess where they came from and what they mean. But with other idioms, you can sometimes figure out their meaning. See if you can guess what the following idiom means. Also, try to describe a scenario when you might use it. Costar un ojo de la cara

Solution:

This expression means that something is very expensive. It is similar to the English expression "cost an arm and a leg." People might use this expression when shopping if they believe that prices are exorbitant. Before discussing the solution, encourage students to share their thoughts and explore different interpretations of the expression.

Standards Targeted: 1.1, 1.2, 1.3, and 4.1

135. La última gota...

Preparation:

Make copies of the following drawing or display on a projector.

Versión 1:	Versión 2:
El siguiente dibujo representa el dicho "La última gota que hace rebosar la copa." Usando el dibujo y tu conocimiento del español, ¿qué piensas que significa este dicho? ¿Cómo lo usarías?	Look at the following drawing. It illustrates the expression "La última gota que hace rebosar la copa." Using the drawing and your knowledge of Spanish, what do you think the expression means? How might it be used?

Solution:

Literally translated, this expression means "The last drop that causes the cup to overflow." It is used in the same way as the English expression, "The straw that broke the camel's back." It means that something is the final burden that someone cannot take.

Variations and Additional Activities:

Provide students with a list of dichos (try to find ones that correspond with topics in your curriculum). Ask students to create drawings explaining the dichos. Then, use the students' drawing for future warm up problems with your class. Also, display the images in your room.

Standards Targeted: 1.1, 1.2, 1.3, and 4.1

"La última gota que hace rebosar la copa."

136. ¿Hay moros en la costa?

Versión 1:	Versión 2:
Los españoles usan el dicho "¿Hay moros en la costa?" para preguntar si hay algún peligro cerca. En inglés hay un dicho similar "Is the coast clear?"	People from Spain often use the expression "¿Hay moros en la costa?" to ask if there is any danger nearby. The English expression "Is the coast clear?" is very similar.
Piensa sobre la historia de España. ¿De dónde crees que viene este dicho?	Think about the history of Spain. Where do you think this expression could have come from?

Solution:

Spain was controlled by the Moors from 711 until 1492. Prior to the complete expulsion of the Moors from Spain, there were pirate Moors who would travel around the Mediterranean coast and capture people for ransom or to rob them. Sometimes they would also attack towns. Guards would patrol the coastlines (often from towers) and signal to people if any pirates were spotted by shouting "Hay moros en la costa." The guards would also ring bells to alert the people to defend themselves. Now this expression is used to signal danger.

Variations and Additional Activities:

Only five dichos are included in this text, however there are many dichos that you could use to enrich and supplement your curriculum. Furthermore, there are many ways to present dichos to your students and encourage that students use them regularly. Consider using additional expressions as part of future warmup problems. You could present them using one of the five strategies featured in this text or using a different strategy.

Additional dichos to consider teaching students:

Dicho:	Basic meaning:
Echar agua al mar	Something that is pointless
Como dos gotas de agua	When two things are very similar
Estar entre la espada y la pared	To be in a difficult situation (much like the English expression "between a rock and a hard place")
Tener mala pata	To have bad luck
En boca cerrado no entran moscas	It is best to keep quiet
Lo barato sale caro	Something cheap often turns out to be expensive
Lloviendo a cántaros	Heavy rain (much like the English expressions "raining cats and dogs" or "raining buckets")

Standards Targeted: 1.1, 1.2, 1.3, and 4.1

Actividades visuales

Puzzles and activities that require students to think visually

137. Dibujos de palabras

Preparation:

Copy the word pictures included on the next page. If you prefer, you can display the word pictures using a projector.

Versión 1:	Versión 2:
Los siguientes dibujos representan palabras. Intenta averiguar qué palabras son.	The following pictures represent different words. Try to figure out what words are drawn.

Presentation Suggestion:

If possible, create word pictures for the vocabulary you are studying or want to review with students. Consider developing a file of word pictures for the chapters you teach so that you can easily access pictures featuring your chapter vocabulary.

Solution:

1. Botella
2. Pantalla
3. La planta baja
4. Hola

Standards Targeted: 1.1, 1.2, and 1.3

138. Tus dibujos de palabras

Preparation:

Copy the word pictures included on the next page. If you prefer, you can display the word pictures using a projector. If you did #138 previously, students may remember the word pictures and not need to see them displayed again.

Versión 1:	Versión 2:
Haz un dibujo o varios dibujos para representar una palabra de tu vocabulario.	Create a picture or series of pictures to represent a vocabulary word from this chapter.

Presentation Suggestion:

After students create their vocabulary pictures, have them trade pages with a partner. Then, their partners need to decipher what the pictures represent. Beginning students can create simple pictures of their vocabulary words. For more advanced students, encourage or require them to use multiple images in their pictures and have them create pictures for phrases or sentences.

Standards Targeted: 1.1, 1.2, and 1.3

Dibujos de palabras

Example:

 $- H =$ limonada

(limón)   (hada)

1.

 $-as +$ $=$

2.

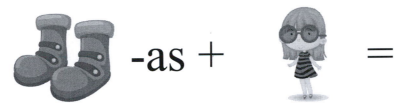 $+$ $=$

3.   **4.**

 $H +$ $=$

139. ¿Qué será?

Preparation:

Copy the student sheet. The students need to follow the directions in order to plot points on the graph. Then, they will connect those points to reveal a picture.

Presentation Suggestion:

Instead of having all of the students complete this activity using the written directions, you could turn this into a communicative activity between partners. Give half of the students the solution and half of the students the graph without the directions. The students with the solution must tell their partners where to plot the points using only Spanish directions.

Solution:

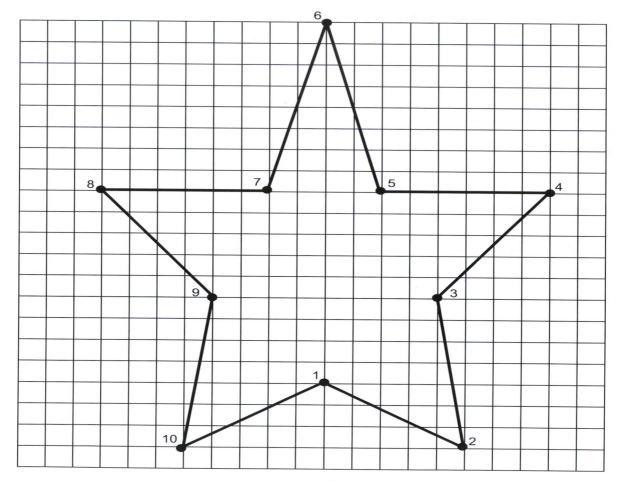

Standards Targeted: 1.1, 1.2, and 1.3

¿Qué será?

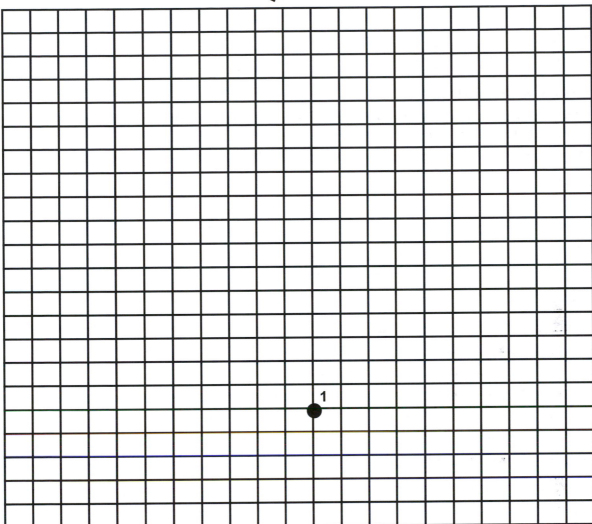

Instrucciones:

1. Empieza en el punto con el número 1.

2. Ve 5 espacios a la derecha y 4 espacios abajo. Pon un punto; escribe "2."

3. Ve 8 espacios arriba y un espacio a la izquierda. Pon un punto; escribe "3."

4. Ve 5 espacios arriba y 4 espacios a la derecha. Pon un punto; escribe "4."

5. Ve 6 espacios a la izquierda. Pon un punto; escribe el número "5."

6. Ve 8 espacios arriba y 2 espacios a la izquierda. Pon un punto; escribe "6."

7. Ve 8 espacios abajo y 2 espacios a la izquierda. Pon un punto; escribe "7."

8. Ve 6 espacios a la izquierda. Pon un punto; escribe "8."

9. Ve 5 espacios abajo y 4 espacios a la derecha. Pon un punto; escribe "9."

10. Ve 8 espacios abajo y un espacio a la izquierda. Pon un punto; escribe "10."

11. Conecta los puntos en orden (conecta el 10 con el 1). ¿Qué figura tienes?

140. ¿Qué será? II

Preparation:

Copy the following student sheet. The students need to follow the directions in order to plot points on the graph. Then they will connect those points to reveal a picture.

Presentation Suggestion:

Instead of having all of the students complete this activity using the written directions, you could turn this into a communicative activity between partners. Give half of the students the solution and half of the students the graph without the directions. The students with the solution must tell their partners where to plot the points using only Spanish directions.

Solution:

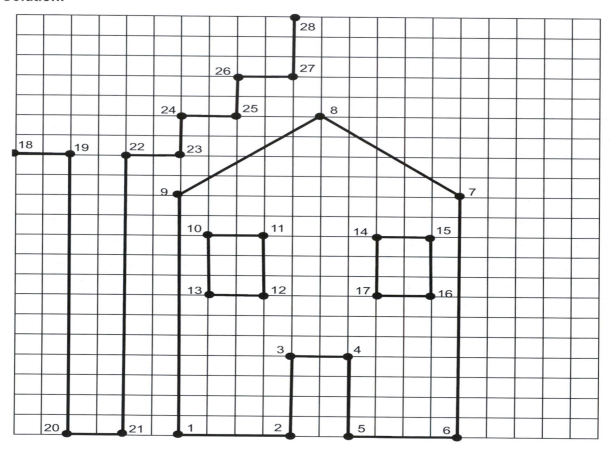

Variations and Additional Activities:

A blank chart is included on page 180. Have students create their own pictures on the graph. The students should then write directions for a partner so that their partners can recreate the image without seeing it. This activity can be done in orally or as a written assignment. If completed orally, encourage students to ask each other questions and engage in a Spanish conversation.

Standards Targeted: 1.1, 1.2, and 1.3

¿Qué será? II

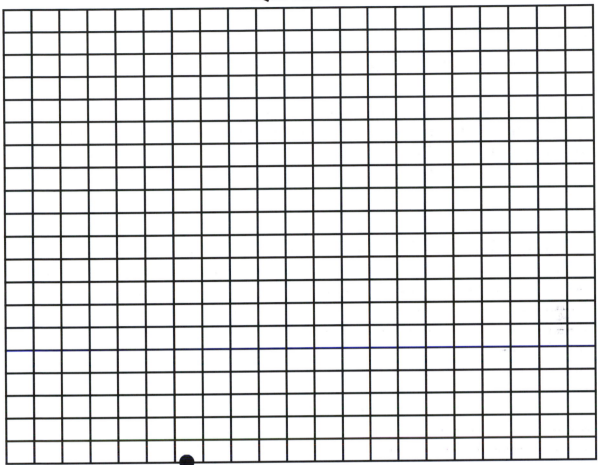

Direcciones: Para cada número ve al espacio indicado. Pun un punto e también escribe el número.

1. Empieza en número 1.
2. Ve 4 espacios a la derecha (pon un punto, escribe #2).
3. Ve arriba 4 espacios.
4. Ve 2 espacios a la derecha.
5. Ve abajo 4 espacios.
6. Ve 4 espacios a la derecha.
7. Ve arriba 11 espacios.
8. Ve 5 espacios a la izquierda y 4 espacios arriba.
9. Ve 5 espacios a la izquierda y 4 espacios abajo.
10. Ve 2 espacios abajo y un espacio a la derecha.
11. Ve 2 espacios a la derecha.
12. Ve 3 espacios abajo.
13. Ve 2 espacios a la izquierda.
14. Ve 6 espacios a la derecha.
15. Ve 2 espacios a la derecha.
16. Ve 3 espacios arriba.
17. Ve 2 espacios a la izquierda.
18. Ve 13 espacios a la izquierda y 4 espacios arriba.
19. Ve 2 espacios a la derecha.
20. Ve 13 espacios abajo.
21. Ve 2 espacios a la derecha.
22. Ve 13 espacios arriba.
23. Ve 2 espacios a la derecha.
24. Ve 2 espacios arriba.
25. Ve 2 espacios a la derecha.
26. Ve 2 espacios arriba.
27. Ve 2 espacios a la derecha.
28. Ve 3 espacios arriba.
29. Conecta números 1–9. También conecta número 9 a 1.
30. Conecta números 10–13. También conecta número 10 a 13.
31. Conecta números 14–17. También conecta número 17–14.
32. Conecta números 18–28.

¿Qué será?

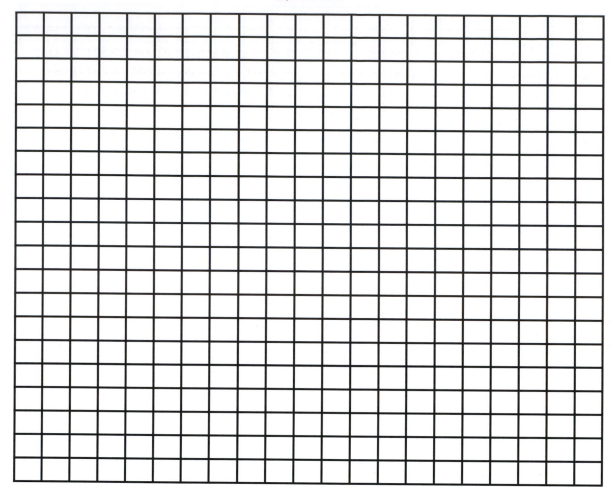

141. Pictogramas

| Versión 1: | Versión 2: |

Versión 1:

Hoy vas a crear un dibujo con palabras. Puedes usar las letras de la palabra o puedes hacer dibujos alrededor de las letras para demostrar que significa la palabra. También puedes escribir las letras artísticamente. Sé creativo.

Ejemplos:

1. fruta (fruit)

2. cuadrado (square)

3. caliente (hot)

Versión 2:

A pictogram is a drawing created in, around, or using the letters of a word. Create pictograms using your vocabulary words.

Ejemplos:

1. fruta (fruit)

2. cuadrado (square)

3. caliente (hot)

Presentation Suggestion:

If possible, provide students with blank paper and art supplies (colored pencils, markers, rulers) to create their pictograms. After students create the pictograms, you can photocopy them onto one or two sheets of papers and distribute them to the whole class so that students could use them to study their vocabulary. The images can really help students remember their words!

Standards Targeted: 1.1, 1.2, and 1.3

142. Arte de palabras

Versión 1:	Versión 2:
Hoy vas a hacer un dibujo pero no puedes dibujar líneas ni otras figuras. Lo que tienes que hacer es usar palabras para hacer tu dibujo. Por ejemplo, si quieres dibujar una nube, puedes escribir la palabra "nube" en la forma de una nube. O puedes escribir la palabra muchas veces usando las palabras para crear tu dibujo.	Today you are going to draw a picture but you cannot draw any lines or shapes. What you have to do is write words to create your picture! If you want to draw a cloud, then use the word "nube" written in the shape of a cloud. You can write the word repeatedly or you can make the whole word the shape of a cloud and write it only once.

Ejemplo:

Presentation Suggestion:

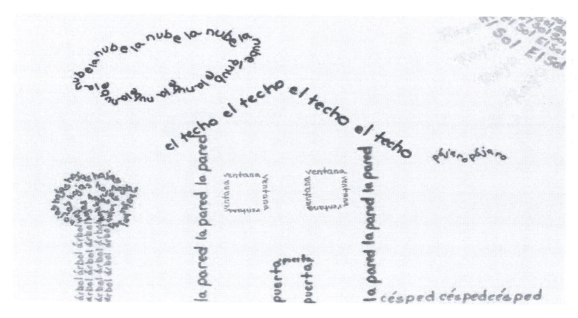

You may want to copy the sample onto an overhead sheet so that all the students can see it.

For this activity, consider providing blank paper and colored pencils or markers for students to work with. In a short amount of time (about five minutes), students should be able to complete a simple drawing. However, some students may enjoy the activity and might want to create a more elaborate drawing. They could continue the picture as homework.

You may want to require that students complete their pictures using the vocabulary you are currently studying. Some topics are more conducive to creating word art, such as food, houses, clothing, body, or animals.

Standards Targeted: 1.1, 1.2, and 1.3

Beginnings and Endings

Activities that teach students about prefixes and suffixes

The following five exercises teach students about prefixes and suffixes. You may want to do them in order, or in a set pattern such as one each Friday. Encourage students to keep their answers to these exercises together in a binder or folder. Students can refer to this work in their future as they continue studying Spanish.

143. Prefijos I

Versión 1:	Versión 2:
Aprendiendo prefijos puede ayudarte a mejorar tu vocabulario y averiguar el significado de palabras nuevas. Mira la siguiente lista de palabras e intenta averiguar qué significa cada prefijo. También necesitas intentar pensar en otra palabra con el mismo prefijo.	Knowing a variety of prefixes can increase your vocabulary and help you understand new words. Look at the list of words below and see if you can figure out what each prefix means. Then try to think of another word with the same prefix.

Prefijo:	Ejemplo:	Prefijo:	Ejemplo:
ante-	anteayer	ante-	anteayer
anti-	antiácido	anti-	antiácido
cent-	centímetro	cent-	centímetro
ex-	exportar	ex-	exportar
in-	incómodo	in-	incómodo
mono-	monolingüe	mono-	monolingüe
pre-	prefijo	pre-	prefijo
pro-	proclamar	pro-	proclamar
super-	supermercado	super-	supermercado
tele-	telegrama	tele-	telegrama

Presentation Suggestion:

Many students might not know all of the sample words. Before students use a dictionary, encourage them to try to guess what the words mean as many of them are cognates. Similarly, encourage students to think of other words with the same prefixes before they look at a dictionary. If students do use a dictionary to find additional words, remind them to check the meaning of their new words carefully as not all words that appear to start with those prefixes actually follow the meaning.

Modify the prefixes you feature in this activity to fit with your curriculum and your students' needs and interests.

Solution:

Prefijo:	Ejemplo:	Significado	Más ejemplos
ante-	Anteayer (yesterday)	Before	Anteanoche, anteceder, antenatal, anteponer
anti-	Antiácido (antacid)	Against	Antiarrugas, antibiótico, antipático, antivirus
cent-	Centímetro (centimeter)	One hundred	Centavo, centenario, centésimo, centígrado

ex-	Exportar (to export)	Outside/former	Exalumno, excavar, exclamar, expatriado
in-	Incómodo (uncomfortable)	Opposite/un-	Inaplicable, inatento, incapaz, independiente
mono-	Monolingüe (monolingual)	One	Monocarril, monocromo, monóculo, monopatín
pre-	Prefijo (Prefix)	Before	Predeterminar, predisposición, preescolar
pro-	Proclamar (to proclaim)	In favor of/forward	Progreso, prometer, promoción, promover
super-	Supermercado (supermarket)	Superior/above	Superconductor, superfluo, superlativo, superponer
tele-	Telegrama (telegram)	At a distance (now also used to express via television/phone)	Telecompra, teléfono, telepatía, telescopio, televisión

Standards Targeted: 1.1, 1.2, 1.3, 3.1, 3.2, and 4.1

144. Prefijos II

Versión 1:	Versión 2:
Aprendiendo prefijos puede ayudarte a mejorar tu vocabulario y averiguar el significado de palabras nuevas. Lee las siguientes descripciones e intenta escribir un prefijo con ese significado. Intenta también escribir una palabra que usa cada prefijo.	Knowing a variety of prefixes can increase your vocabulary and help you understand new words. Read the following descriptions and try to think of a prefix with that meaning. Also, try to think of a sample word for each prefix.

Versión 1:

1. Para si mismo
2. Uno
3. Muchos
4. Debajo
5. Dos
6. De nuevo/otra vez
7. No bueno/malo
8. Entre/en
9. Deshacer/disminuir
10. Mitad/no completamente

Versión 2:

1. Self
2. One
3. Many
4. Under/below
5. Two
6. Again/with greater intensity
7. Bad
8. Among/between
9. Undo/diminish
10. Partially/Medium

Presentation Suggestion:

Many students might not know all of the sample words. Before students use a dictionary, encourage them to try to guess what the words mean as many of them are cognates. Similarly, encourage students to think of other words with the same prefixes before they look at a dictionary. If students do use a dictionary to find additional words, remind them to check the meaning of their new words carefully as not all words that appear to start with those prefixes actually follow the meaning.

Solution:

#	Descripción	Prefijo	Ejemplos
1	Para si mismo	Auto-	Autoanálisis, autobiografía, autocracia, autodefensa
2	Uno	Uni-	Unicelular, unicornio, unidireccional, unificar
3	Muchos	Poli-	Polifacético, poligloto, polígono, polisílabo, politeísmo
4	Debajo	Sub-	Subconsciente, submarino, subrayar, subtítulo
5	Dos	Bi-/bis-	Bicicleta, binoculares, bisabuelo, bisemanal, bisílabo
6	De nuevo/otra vez	Re-	Reafirmar, recomendar, repasar, reiterar, rellenar
7	No bueno/malo	Mal-	Malcriar, malévolo, malgastar, malnutrido, maltratar
8	Entre/en	Inter-	Interactivo, intercambiar, intermedio, internacional, internet
9	Deshacer/disminuir	De-/des-	Desacuerdo, desafortunado, desaparecer, desordenado
10	Mitad/no completamente	Semi-	Semicírculo, semiconductor, semifinal, semiseco

Standards Targeted: 1.1, 1.2, 1.3, 3.1, 3.2, and 4.1

145. Using suffixes to make new words

Preparation:

Because the directions are somewhat lengthy, the following activity is included as a separate handout. You can make copies of the handout or can display the instructions on a projector or the board.

Presentation Suggestion:

In this exercise, students are asked to change words by following suffix patterns. Sometimes, students take patterns or trends and believe they can apply these patterns to everything. However, these patterns are not rules and they cannot be applied to all words. Remind students that knowing these patterns and learning the suffixes will help them improve their Spanish, but they should not overapply this knowledge! Also, when students try to create a new word by following the patterns, encourage their attempts while also recommending that they use another source to verify that their new word actually exists. (You can end up with a classroom full of students saying things like, "Necesito tu ayudación" or "Trabajo buenamente.")

Modify the examples to fit with your curriculum. Select words that will appropriately challenge your students.

Solution:

adjetivo	➡	adverbio
frecuente		frecuentemente
rápido		rápidamente
natural		naturalmente
exacto		exactamente

verbo	➡	sustantivo
celebrar		celebración
comunicar		comunicación
declarar		declaración
explorar		exploración
meditar		meditación
participar		participación

Standards Targeted: 1.1, 1.2, 1.3, 3.1, 3.2, and 4.1

Using suffixes to make new words (versión 1)

Otra manera de mejorar tu vocabulario y comprender palabras nuevas es usando sufijos. Puedes usar el sufijo "-mente" para crear adverbios de adjetivos (usa la forma singular y femenino).

Ejemplo:

adjetivo ➡ adverbio   loving ➡ lovingly

Tu turno: (no te olvides de usar la forma singular y femenina)

adjetivo ➡	adverbio	adjetivo ➡	adverbio
frecuente	_____	natural	_____
rápido	_____	exacto	_____

Palabras que terminan en "-ción" generalmente son sustantivos. A veces puedes tomar un verbo (normalmente -ar) y cambiarlo a un sustantivo.

Ejemplo:

verbo ➡ sustantivo   actuar ➡ actuación

Tu turno:

verbo ➡	sustantivo	verbo ➡	sustantivo
celebrar	_____	explorar	_____
comunicar	_____	meditar	_____
declarar	_____	participar	_____

Using suffixes to make new words (versión 2)

Using suffixes is another great way to expand your vocabulary and understand new words. The ending "-mente" can be used to turn adjectives (use feminine singular) into adverbs.

Ejemplo:

adjective ➡ adverb   loving ➡ lovingly

Your turn: (remember to use the feminine-singular form!)

adjetivo ➡	adverbio	adjetivo ➡	adverbio
frecuente	_____	natural	_____
rápido	_____	exacto	_____

Words that end in "-ción" are usually nouns. Sometimes you can take a verb (usually -ar) and transform it into a noun.

Ejemplo:

verbo ➡ sustantivo   actuar ➡ actuación

Tu turno:

verbo ➡	sustantivo	verbo ➡	sustantivo
celebrar	_____	explorar	_____
comunicar	_____	meditar	_____
declarar	_____	participar	_____

146. Suffixes and Sizes

Versión 1:	Versión 2:
Podemos usar sufijos para expresar tamaño. Para expresar que algo es pequeño agregamos "-ito/a." Para expresar que algo es grande agregamos "-ón," "-ona," "-ote," o "-ota." La forma diminutiva (para expresar que algo es más pequeño) es muy común y también se usa para expresar cariño.	You can use suffixes to help express something's size. To express that something is *small* you add "-ito/a". When expressing something is *large* you add "-ón," "-ona," "-ote" or "-ota." The diminutive (used to express that something is small) is very common and can also be used as a term of endearment.
Ejemplos:	**Ejemplos:**
The name "Jorgito" is the diminutive of "Jorge" or little George.	The name "Jorgito" is the diminutive of "Jorge" or little George.
Taza = cup	Taza = cup
Tazita = little cup	Tazita = little cup
Tazón = big cup or often the term for bowl	Tazón = big cup or often the term for bowl
Tu turno: Ahora intenta pensar en más ejemplos que conoces o que puedes usar.	Your turn: Now, try to think of diminutives or augmentatives you know or might use.

Additional Information:

Other diminutives or augmentatives are used in different countries or regions. For example, in southern Spain "-illo/a" is a very common diminutive. To avoid confusing students, only a few diminutives and augmentatives are presented here. Feel free to use other forms as you see fit.

Solution:

Students answers will vary. Encourage students to think about when they have encountered diminutives and augmentatives (even if they didn't know those terms yet). Also, encourage students to try and use those suffixes with their vocabulary words when appropriate.

Standards Targeted: 1.1, 1.2, 1.3, 3.1, 3.2, and 4.1

147. Suffixes and Cognates

Versión 1:	Versión 2:
Muchos sufijos ingleses corresponden con sufijos españoles. Intenta llenar los cuadros vacios del siguiente gráfico.	Many English suffixes correspond to Spanish suffixes. Try to fill in the empty spaces on the chart below.

Sufijo en español	Sufijo en inglés	Ejemplo en español	Ejemplo en inglés
-arquía		Monarquía	
-ático		Acuático	Aquatic
-cida/-cidio		Pesticida	Pesticide
	-tion		Nation
-cracia	-cracy	Democracia	Democracy
-dad			Activity
	-phobia		Claustrophobia
-fono		Teléfono	
-ificar		Clasificar	Classify
-ismo	-ism		Pessimism
	-ist		Cyclist

Presentation Suggestion:

Consider photocopying the chart for students so they can fill it in more quickly.

Solution:

Sufijo en español	Sufijo en inglés	Ejemplo en español	Ejemplo en inglés
-arquía	-archy	Monarquía	Monarchy
-ático	-atic	Acuático	Aquatic
-cida/-cidio	-cide	Pesticida	Pesticide
-ción	-tion	Nación	Nation
-cracia	-cracy	Democracia	Democracy
-dad	-ity	Actividad	Activity
-fobia	-phobia	Claustrofobia	Claustrophobia
-fono	-phono	Teléfono	Telephone
-ificar	-ify	Clasificar	Classify
-ismo	-ism	Pesimismo	Pessimism
-ista	-ist	Ciclista	Cyclist

Standards Targeted: 1.1, 1.2, 1.3, 3.1, 3.2, and 4.1®